Cordon Bleu

Baking 2

Cordon Bleu

Baking 2

Pies, Tarts and Pastries

CBC / B.P.C. Publishing Ltd.

Published by
B.P.C. Publishing Ltd.,
P.O. Box 20,
Abingdon, Oxon.

© B.P.C. Publishing Ltd., 1971.

Designed by Melvyn Kyte
Printed and bound in England
by Waterlow (Dunstable) Limited

These recipes have been adapted from the Cordon Bleu Cookery Course
published by Purnell in association with the London Cordon Bleu Cookery
School
Principal: Rosemary Hume; Co-Principal: Muriel Downes
Spoon measures are level unless otherwise stated.

Contents

Introduction

Any cook worth her salt must be able to make pastry—and it is surprising how many people can't. In fact, attention to just a few details can ensure good results every time and the first part of this book is devoted to the basic rules and recipes for good pastry.

But having learnt to make pastry, the great art is in filling it! In Britain these days, we are rather conservative about pies and tarts—our repertoire is strictly limited to a few traditional favourites. But we should take a tip from our grandmothers and great-grandmothers—they knew that their reputations as cooks hung on the quality and variety of the pies they could turn out.

The Americans too seem to specialize in unusual pies—the varied backgrounds of the settlers brought together many different baking traditions, which have blended until the origins are well obscured, and the result is truly American and well worth imitation.

European gâteaux and pâtisseries are a very different, highly specialised form of pastry work. In Paris or Vienna few housewives will make their own, for the professionally made ones are so good they cannot hope to better them. In Britain, however, it is not always possible to obtain the real thing, so it is well worth trying to master the art of producing some of the simpler confections.

Large and small, sweet and savoury, pies, flans and pastries are just the thing for family cooking and entertaining. And if you have a home freezer, don't forget that you can save time by making a large batch of pastry at once and freezing in pies and tarts for future use. Freeze them baked or unbaked in aluminium foil dishes (though many people consider that the baked version freezes best).

Apart from the section on pastry making, we have included in this book an appendix—a glossary of cooking terms and notes on the preparation of various items that recur throughout the book. Experienced cooks may not need to use this, but if there is anything you do not understand in a recipe, you will probably find it explained in the appendix. And experienced or not, we hope you will find something new to add to your baking repertoire.

Rosemary Hume
Muriel Downes

Pastry making

How to make pastry

Good pastry is not difficult to make if certain rules — which are often forgotten — are followed. The main points are:

1 Work in a cool, airy room. Plan to make the pastry before the kitchen becomes warm from other cooking because a damp, warm atmosphere is disastrous.

2 Use fresh, fine-sifted plain flour (self-raising flour or baking powder produces spongy-textured pastry), firm but not hard fat (which would not blend properly with the flour) and ice-cold water for mixing. Baking powder is sometimes used to lighten a rich pastry that has a lot of fat.

3 Handle flour and fat lightly but firmly. When rubbing fat into the flour, keep lifting it up and crumbling the mixture between your fingers. This movement helps to aerate the dough. Shake the bowl after 1-2 minutes to bring the larger lumps of fat to the surface and to show you how much more rubbing-in is necessary. This is especially helpful when making rich short-crust where over-rubbing makes the pastry greasy.

4 Make sure that the correct amount of water is added. This may vary a little with the quality of the flour. Too dry a mixture makes the pastry dough difficult to handle; it will crack when rolled out and crumble after baking and will be dry to eat. Too wet a dough will shrink and lose shape while baking, and also makes for tough, hard pastry. The amount of water is usually indicated in a recipe and it is important that at least two-thirds of the given quantity are added to the dry ingredients

How to make pastry

continued

before mixing begins. This avoids overworking and brings the ingredients quickly to a firm, smooth dough, especially when making the foundation for puff pastry.

5 A marble slab or slate shelf is ideal for rolling out pastry dough because it is smooth, solid and cool; otherwise, keep a board especially for this purpose (a laminated plastic surface is cool). Once dough is rolled out, always scrape slab or board thoroughly before rolling out new dough to remove any pieces that may have stuck and which might cause further sticking. (This applies particularly to flaky or puff pastry when rolling out is of paramount importance.) Use a minimum amount of flour for dusting when rolling, otherwise too much will go into the pastry dough and spoil it. A heavy, plain wooden rolling pin without handles is best, especially for puff pastry.

6 Chill made pastry dough for

Note: when terms such as '8 oz of pastry' or 'an 8 oz quantity of pastry' are used, this means the amount obtained by using 8 oz of flour, not 8 oz of prepared pastry dough. As a quantity guide, 8 oz of flaky or rough puff pastry will cover a 9-inch long pie dish, or an 8-inch diameter pie plate.

about 30 minutes or leave it aside in a cool place for the same amount of time. This gives dough a chance to relax and removes any elasticity which may cause shrinkage round edge of dish.

7 It is essential when baking pastry to pre-set the oven to the required temperature. The immediate heat sets the pastry in its correct shape and makes it possible to control the exact amount of cooking time.

Shortcrust pastry

For shortcrust pastry the basic proportions of ingredients are half the amount of fat to the weight of flour, and ¼ oz salt to each lb flour. For rich short-crust, allow 2 egg yolks to every lb flour. When more fat is added, as in many recipes using rich shortcrust, the pastry is shorter (ie. lighter and more crisp), and is best for pies and tarts to be eaten cold. Butter, margarine, lard or shortening (one of the commercially prepared cooking fats) may be used. A mixture of fats gives the best results, eg. butter and lard, as the former gives a good flavour and the latter a good texture.

Basic recipe

8 oz plain flour
pinch of salt
4-6 oz butter, margarine, lard or
    shortening, or mixture of any two
3-4 tablespoons cold water

Method

Sift the flour with a pinch of salt into a mixing bowl. Cut the fat into the flour with a round-bladed knife and, as soon as the pieces are well coated with flour, rub in with fingers until mixture looks like fine breadcrumbs.

Make a well in the centre, add the water (reserving about 1 tablespoon) and mix quickly with a knife. Press together with the fingers, adding the extra water, if necessary, to give a firm dough.

Turn on to a floured board, knead pastry dough lightly until smooth. Chill in refrigerator (wrapped in greaseproof paper, a polythene bag or foil) for 30 minutes before using.

Rich shortcrust pastry

8 oz plain flour
pinch of salt
6 oz butter
1 rounded dessertspoon caster
    sugar (for sweet pastry)
1 egg yolk
2-3 tablespoons cold water

Method

Sift the flour with a pinch of salt into a mixing bowl. Drop in the butter and cut it into the flour until the small pieces are well coated. Then rub them in with the fingertips until the mixture looks like fine breadcrumbs. Stir in the sugar, mix egg yolk with water, tip into the fat and flour and mix quickly with a palette knife to a firm dough.

Turn on to a floured board and knead lightly until smooth. If possible, chill in refrigerator (wrapped in greaseproof paper, a polythene bag or foil) for 30 minutes before using.

Savoury shortcrust pastry

4 oz plain flour
salt and pepper
pinch of cayenne pepper
2 oz shortening
½ oz Parmesan cheese (grated)
½ egg yolk (mixed with 1
  tablespoon water)

Use this pastry for canapés, small boat moulds and tartlet tins.

This quantity will make about twelve 1¼-inch diameter canapés, or fill 12-16 boat moulds or tartlet tins.

Method
Sift the flour with seasonings, rub the shortening into the flour until the mixture resembles breadcrumbs. Add the cheese and mix to a dough with the egg yolk and water.

Chill the pastry dough for 30 minutes before using. Roll out to ¼ inch thick and stamp into rounds 1¼ inches in diameter.

Place on a baking sheet lined with greaseproof paper, or line the dough into boat moulds or tartlet tins. Bake for 7-8 minutes in a moderate oven, pre-set at 375°F or Mark 5.

Watchpoint It is most important not to put this type of cheese pastry direct on to the baking sheet, for such small canapés can easily become scorched in a very short time— in fact in the time that it would take you to lift the first half dozen from your baking sheet. By lifting the greaseproof paper lining straight from the hot baking sheet to a cooling rack you can remove all the canapés from the heat at once.

Savoury almond pastry

4 oz plain flour
salt and pepper
pinch of cayenne pepper
2 oz shortening
½ oz almonds (ground)
½ egg yolk (mixed with 1
  tablespoon water)

Method
Make as for savoury shortcrust (see recipe, left), adding the ground almonds after the shortening has been rubbed into the flour. Chill for 30 minutes before using.

If using for canapés, roll the pastry to ¼-inch thickness and stamp into rounds 1¼ inches in diameter. Put on a baking sheet lined with greaseproof paper, and bake for 7-8 minutes in a moderate oven, pre-set at 375°F or Mark 5.

American pie pastry

Pastry for the American covered pie is slightly different from shortcrust both in ingredients and method. Most recipes for American shortcrust have a high proportion of fat to flour, and usually need more liquid for binding. This is because American and Canadian flour is milled from hard wheat which is very high in gluten (the major part of the protein content of wheat flour, which gives it its elasticity), and consequently absorbs more liquid.

The following recipe is an anglicised version, but has the same short, melt-in-the-mouth texture. As the texture is very short, the pastry is not easy to handle once cooked, so serve the pie in the dish in which it is baked (a round, shallow tin or dish—pie plate—about 2-2½ inches deep). The pastry is lined into the pie plate, the filling is poured on top, and the pie is covered with a lid of pastry.

Basic recipe

8 oz self-raising flour
5 oz lard, or shortening
pinch of salt
2 tablespoons cold water

Method

Place the lard or shortening in a bowl, add a good pinch of salt and the water, and cream ingredients together. Sift the flour over the softened fat and, using a round-bladed knife, cut the fat into the flour and mix to a rough dough. Chill for 30 minutes

Turn the dough on to a floured board, knead lightly and then use for covered fruit pies.

Rough puff pastry

The· first of the two types of rough puff pastry is a quicker and less fussy one, although the same ingredients are used in both types. You can use either type in recipes but the second is likely to be a little lighter.

Basic recipe 1

8 oz plain flour
pinch of salt
6 oz firm butter, or margarine
¼ pint ice-cold water (to mix)

Method

Sift the flour with salt into a mixing bowl. Cut the fat in even-size pieces about the size of walnuts and drop into the flour. Mix quickly with the water (to prevent overworking dough so that it becomes starchy) and turn on to a lightly floured board.

Roll to an oblong, fold in three and make a half-turn to bring the open edges in front of you. Complete this action three times so that the pastry dough has three turns in all. Finally, chill for 10 minutes and give an extra roll and fold if it looks at all streaky, then use as required. ▶

Rough puff pastry continued

Basic recipe 2

8 oz plain flour
pinch salt
6 oz firm butter, or margarine
¼ pint ice-cold water (to mix)

Method

Sift the flour with salt into a mixing bowl. Take 1 oz of the fat and rub it into the flour. Mix to a firm but pliable dough with the water, knead lightly until smooth, then set in a cool place for 10-15 minutes.

Place the remaining fat between two pieces of grease-proof paper and beat to a flat cake with the rolling pin. This fat should be the same consistency as the dough.

Roll out the dough to a rectangle, place the flattened fat in the middle, fold like a parcel and turn over.

Roll out dough to an oblong, fold in three and make a half-turn to bring the open edge towards you. Complete this action three times so that the pastry has three turns in all. Finally chill for 10 minutes, then roll out and use as required.

Flaky pastry

8 oz plain flour
pinch of salt
3 oz butter
3 oz lard
¼ pint ice-cold water (to mix)

Method

Sift the flour with salt into a bowl. Divide the fats into four portions (two of butter, two of lard); rub one portion—either lard or butter—into the flour and mix to a firm dough with cold water. The amount of water varies with different flour but an average quantity for 8 oz flour is 4-5 fluid oz (about ¼ pint or 8-10 tablespoons); the finer the flour the more water it will absorb.

Knead the dough lightly until smooth, then roll out to an oblong. Put a second portion of fat (not the same kind as first portion rubbed in) in small pieces on to two-thirds of the dough. Fold in three, half turn the dough to bring the open edge towards you and roll out again to an oblong. Put on a third portion of fat in pieces, fold dough in three, wrap in a cloth or polythene bag and leave in a cool place for 15 minutes.

Roll out dough again, put on remaining fat in pieces, fold and roll as before. If dough looks at all streaky, give one more turn and roll again.

1 *To make flaky pastry, mix flour and one portion of fat to a firm dough with a little ice-cold water*
2 *Roll out dough to an oblong, dot second portion of fat over two-thirds of dough. Fold in three, half turn and roll out. Repeat, then cool*
3 *Roll dough again, put on last portion of fat and roll out as before*

Puff pastry

Forming the dough

For perfect results when making puff pastry, you must use the right kind of flour and fat, and always use ice-cold water for mixing.

It is also important to work in a very cool atmosphere. Never attempt to make puff pastry in very hot weather; it will become sticky and difficult to handle. Make it early in the morning (if possible before you have done any cooking), as a kitchen soon becomes warm and steamy.

Fat should be cool and firm. The best puff pastry for flavour and texture is made from butter; this should be of a firm consistency and slightly salted—such as English, Australian or New Zealand. Continental butters are too creamy in texture and result in a sticky pastry, difficult to handle.

If margarine has to be used, again use a firm variety (one that does not spread easily). The cheapest varieties of butter and margarine are the best for this purpose.

Flour should be 'strong', ie. a bread flour which has a high gluten content. It should also be well sifted and quite cool.

The flour is made into a firm dough with a little butter and the water. This preliminary mixing is most important as it is on this that the success of the pastry depends.

Add the lemon juice to approximately two-thirds of the given amount of water. Stir until a dough begins to form, then add remaining water. If water is added a little at a time, it ▶ 17

Puff pastry continued

will dry in the flour and the re-sulting dough will be tough. The finished dough should be firm yet pliable and have the consistency of butter, taking into account the different textures.

Knead the dough firmly—this and the presence of the lemon juice develops the gluten in the flour and means that the dough will stand the frequent rolling and folding necessary in the preparation of puff pastry.

The butter should be cool and firm, but not used straight from the refrigerator. If it is over-hard (or not taken from the refrigerator early enough), put it between two pieces of damp greaseproof paper and beat it 2-3 times with the rolling pin. It is then ready to be rolled into the dough.

Rolling out the dough

The method of rolling is also important and differs slightly from the usual way. You roll shortcrust pastry to shape the dough; in puff pastry it is the rolling that actually makes it.

Always roll the dough away from you, keeping the pressure as even as possible. Many people are inclined to put more weight on the right or left hand, which pulls the dough to one side; keep it straight by applying even pressure all round.

Bring the rolling pin down smartly on to the dough and roll it forward with a strong, firm pressure in one direction only. Continue until just before the edge of the dough.
Watchpoint Never let the rolling pin run off the edge as the object is to keep the dough strictly rectangular in shape.

Lift the rolling pin and continue rolling forward in one direction, bringing it down at the point to which it was last rolled. In this way the whole area of the dough is rolled in even layers, ½-¾ inch thick.

Once rolled to an even rectangle, the dough is folded in three round the butter (see method overleaf). Graduate the thickness of the following rollings, so that these subsequent ones are progressively thinner. You must avoid pushing butter through the dough, which might happen if it was rolled thinly in the beginning.
Watchpoint Do not turn the dough over; it should only be rolled on one side.

Each rolling is called a 'turn' and puff pastry usually has six turns with a 15-minute rest between every two. Before each turn the dough is folded in three (ends to middle) and the edges sealed with the side of the hand or the rolling pin to prevent the folds shifting when dough is rolled. The short period of rest is to remove any elasticity from the dough. If at the end of the rollings the dough is at all streaky (showing that the butter has not been rolled in completely), a seventh turn can be given.

Should fat begin to break through dough, stop at once. Dust dough with flour, brush off the surplus, and chill it for 10 minutes before continuing.

Once made, the pastry dough may be finally rolled out, cut to shape and stored, wrapped in greaseproof paper and a cloth. It will keep for 24-48 hours in a cool place.

1 After first rolling out the dough, butter is laid on the centre and sides turned in over it
2 The dough is folded into three, ends to middle, like a parcel

3 The rolling pin is brought down lightly on to the dough to flatten it before rolling out
4 After each rolling, dough is always folded into three

Puff pastry continued

Save all trimmings and fold them in three. Place all trimmings on top of each other. Roll out and use for making mille feuilles, jalousies, palmiers, sacristans (see pages 64-66).

Baking pastry

If the uncooked pastry dough seems a little soft, place it on a baking sheet in refrigerator for about 15 minutes (no longer) for it to firm up before baking.

Place dough on a thick baking sheet well dampened with cold water. This helps to prevent pastry from sliding and shrinking too much while baking. A thick baking sheet will not buckle in the hot oven.

Puff pastry is cooked in a hot oven at 425°F or Mark 7. A large case, such as a vol-au-vent or flan, is baked in the centre of the oven. Small pieces such as bouchées and so on, are baked on the top shelf about 5 inches from the roof of the oven. The above applies to gas ovens, as electric ovens vary according to where the elements are placed. Follow your electric cooker's instruction book.

Basic puff pastry

8 oz plain flour
pinch of salt
8 oz butter
1 teaspoon lemon juice
scant ¼ pint water (ice cold)

This quantity will make a vol-au-vent for 4 people or 6-8 medium-size bouchées. Use up trimmings as recipes on pages 64-66.

Method

Sift flour and salt into a bowl. Rub in a piece of butter the size of a walnut. Add lemon juice to water, make a well in centre of flour and pour in about two-thirds of the liquid. Mix with a palette, or round-bladed knife. When the dough is beginning to form, add remaining water.

Turn out the dough on to a marble slab, a laminated-plastic work top, or a board, dusted with flour. Knead dough for 2-3 minutes, then roll out to a square about ½-¾ inch thick.

Beat butter, if necessary, to make it pliable and place in centre of dough. Fold this up over butter to enclose it completely (sides and ends over centre like a parcel). Wrap in a cloth or piece of greaseproof paper and put in the refrigerator for 10-15 minutes.

Flour slab or work top, put on dough, the join facing upwards, and bring rolling pin down on to dough 3-4 times to flatten it slightly.

Now roll out to a rectangle about ½-¾ inch thick. Fold into three, ends to middle, as accurately as possible, if necessary pulling the ends to keep them rectangular. Seal the edges with your hand or rolling pin and turn dough half round to bring the edge towards you. Roll out again and fold in three (keep a note of the 'turns' given). Set aside in refrigerator for 15 minutes.

Repeat this process, giving a total of 6 turns with a 15-minute rest after each two turns. Then leave in the refrigerator until wanted.

French flan pastry (Pâte sucrée)

French flan pastry is made with plain flour, butter, caster sugar and egg yolks, and no liquid of any kind. The method of making is completely different from English shortcrust pastry and, for this reason, the resulting dough should be firm and completely non-elastic. This means that the pastry keeps its shape during baking and when cooked is slightly short and melt-in-the-mouth. It should be made 1-2 hours before use, then chilled. Take it out of refrigerator 15-20 minutes before you use it and keep it at room temperature.

When cooled, French flan pastry is a delicate biscuit-colour; if over-cooked, it becomes hard and tasteless.

Basic recipe 1

4 oz plain flour
pinch of salt
2 oz butter
2 oz caster sugar
2-3 drops of vanilla essence
2 egg yolks

This quantity is sufficient to line a 7-inch diameter flan ring or 9-12 individual tartlet tins.
Note: 2 oz vanilla sugar may be used instead of caster sugar and vanilla essence.

Method

Sieve the flour with a pinch of salt on to a marble slab or pastry board, make a well in the centre and in it place the butter, sugar, vanilla essence and egg yolks. Using the fingertips of one hand only, pinch and work these last three ingredients together until well blended. Then gradually draw in the flour; knead lightly until smooth.

1 *Make well in flour, put in sugar, yolks, butter and vanilla*
2 *With fingertips of one hand, work all ingredients to a paste*
3 *Draw in flour quickly, kneading lightly until smooth; chill pastry before using*

21

Choux pastry

Choux pastry is not made like other types of pastry. The fat is put into a pan with water and, when this has boiled, the flour is poured in and beaten. It is important, however, that you only beat the flour until the pastry is smooth; this takes a few seconds only. Continued beating at this stage will mean that the pastry will not rise.

Use plain flour, or, for a particularly crisp result, a 'strong' flour (one with a good gluten content). This type of flour is now available in good stores throughout the country.

Once the eggs have been added, the dough should then be beaten thoroughly. An electric mixer can be used at this stage with the paddle or dough hook on slow speed.

Choux pastry should be baked in a hot oven on a rising temperature, ie. cooked for 10 minutes at 400°F or Mark 6, then the cooking completed at 425°F or Mark 7 for the length of time given in the recipe. This will ensure that the choux is brown and crisp. If it is still pale in colour, it will collapse when taken out of the oven.

Choux is usually baked on a dampened baking sheet (hold sheet under the cold tap for a few seconds). Once baked and taken off the sheet to cool, make a hole in the side of the choux pastry with a skewer or the point of knife to release any steam and so keep it crisp.

Do not make more choux pastry than you need. Once baked it does not keep well and should be used within 2-3 hours.

Choux pastry may also be fried; for instructions, see cheese beignets, page 90.

1 *Adding flour to pan after the water and fat have been boiled*
2 *Beating the flour mixture until choux paste is very smooth*
3 *Adding the eggs, one at a time, and beating them in well*

Basic choux pastry

Quantity for 3-4 people
¼ pint (5 fl oz) water
2 oz butter, or margarine
2½ oz plain flour
2 eggs

Quantity for 4-6 people
7½ fl oz water
3 oz butter, or margarine
3¾ oz plain flour
3 eggs

Method

Put water and fat into a fairly large pan. Sift flour on to a piece of paper. Bring contents of the pan to the boil and when bubbling draw pan aside, allow bubbles to subside and pour in all the flour at once. Stir vigorously with a wooden spoon until it is smooth (a few seconds).

Cool mixture for about 5 minutes, then beat in the eggs one at a time. If eggs are large, break the last one into a bowl and beat with a fork. Add this slowly to ensure that the mixture remains firm and keeps its shape (you may not need to use all of this last egg).

Beat pastry dough for about 3 minutes until it looks glossy. It is then ready to be piped out, using a plain éclair nozzle, or shaped with a spoon for baking or frying.

Genoese pastry

This recipe makes a rich, firm type of sponge cake foundation, lighter than the English kind. Although it is called pâte (pastry), it is not a true pastry but traditionally comes under the heading of pâtisseries because it is widely used in this particular field.

Basic recipe 1

4¼ oz plain flour
pinch of salt
2 oz butter
4 eggs
4¼ oz caster sugar

8½-9 inch diameter moule à manqué

Basic recipe 2

3 oz plain flour
pinch of salt
1½ oz butter
3 eggs
3¼ oz caster sugar

7½-8 inch diameter moule à manqué

Method

Set the oven at 350-375°F or Mark 4-5; grease mould, line bottom only with a disc of greaseproof paper to fit exactly, grease again, dust with caster sugar, then flour.

Sift the flour 2 or 3 times with the salt. Warm the butter gently until just soft and pourable, taking great care not to make it hot or oily. Have ready a large saucepan half full of boiling water over which the mixing bowl will rest comfortably without touching the water.

Break the eggs into the bowl

Genoese pastry continued

and beat in the sugar gradually. Remove the saucepan from the heat, place the bowl on top and whisk the eggs and sugar until thick and mousse-like. This will take quite 7-8 minutes and the mixture will increase in volume and lighten in colour; when lifted on the whisk a little will fall back, forming a ribbon on the mixture in the bowl. Remove the bowl from the heat and continue whisking for 5 minutes until mixture is cold. Now, using a metal spoon, very gently cut and fold in two-thirds of the flour,

then the butter, quickly followed by the remaining flour.

Watchpoint If you have an electric mixer, there is no need to place the mixing bowl over hot water but do add the flour by hand, cutting and folding it in as described in the recipe.

Turn the mixture immediately into prepared mould, bake in a pre-set oven for 30-35 minutes.

For genoese pastry, fold in flour by hand, add melted butter and remaining flour before baking in the lined mould

Gâteaux

Be really adventurous next time you have a party, and give your friends a traditional continental gâteau as a dessert. Europe provides a rich store of these delicious gâteaux, the most famous from Vienna, with France not far behind. The names and decorations are traditional, and they should be instantly recognisable wherever you come across them.

For success, attention to detail is vitally important. Scales must be used and, if you consider undertaking this sort of baking fairly frequently, it is worth buying a set of French weights or a set of scales marked with both measuring systems. The necessary accuracy is not always easy to achieve with the avoirdupois system, even with conversion tables.

Many of the recipes use French flan pastry (pâte sucrée) because it stands up better than shortcrust to being filled with fruit and glazed. The quantities given in our recipes will serve 8 people, as these gâteaux can't really be made successfully with less ingredients.

Gâteau St. Honoré

2 oz quantity of French flan
  pastry
1 egg (beaten)
3 egg quantity of choux pastry
2 oz granulated sugar
2 tablespoons water
crème St. Honoré

To decorate

glacé cherries
few diamonds of angelica

Forcing bag, ½-inch plain pipe

Method

Set the oven at 400°F or Mark 6.

Chill French flan pastry dough well, roll it out, ⅛ inch thick, and cut out a round the size of a dessert plate. Place the round on a baking sheet, prick dough well and damp or brush a ½ inch wide band around the edge with beaten egg.

Fill the choux pastry into a forcing bag, and make a circle around edge of French flan pastry. Brush the choux pastry with beaten egg and bake in pre-set oven for about 25 minutes.

Pipe also, on to a baking sheet, 10-15 small rounds of choux pastry about the size of a nut, brush with beaten egg and bake until crisp in pre-set oven for approximately 12-15 minutes.

When choux pastry is cool, dissolve the sugar in the water in a small pan and boil it briskly to 300°F, or until the syrup just begins to turn a pale straw-colour. Dip the bottom of each ball of choux pastry into the sugar syrup and place them close together around the top of the cake. Fill the centre of the cake with the crème St. Honoré and decorate with glacé cherries and diamonds of angelica.

Crème St. Honoré

4 egg yolks
4 oz caster sugar
1 oz plain flour
scant ½ pint milk
vanilla pod
6 egg whites

Method

Cream egg yolks and sugar together until white, add the flour and a little cold milk to make a smooth paste. Scald remaining milk with vanilla pod, then strain this on to egg mixture, blend and return it to pan. Stir over gentle heat until the mixture boils.

Whip egg whites until stiff, turn a little of the boiling custard into a bowl and fold in egg whites. Return this to pan and stir carefully for 2-3 minutes over heat to set egg whites. Turn cream into a bowl to cool.

Top to bottom: gâteau aux groseilles, gâteau moka (see page 28 for these recipes) and gâteau St. Honoré

Gâteau moka

4 egg quantity of genoese pastry
6 oz butter cream (coffee-
flavoured)

To decorate
2 oz almonds (browned and
ground, or finely chopped)
icing sugar (for dredging)

*8½-inch diameter moule à manqué,
or deep 8½-9 inch diameter cake
tin; forcing bag with rose pipe*

Method
Set oven at 350°F or Mark 4.
Prepare the mould or tin by
greasing it, lining the bottom
only with a disc of greaseproof
paper, grease again, dust first
with caster sugar, then with
flour.

Turn the genoese mixture into
mould or tin, then bake in pre-
set oven for approximately
35-40 minutes, or until firm to
the touch. Turn gâteau out and,
when cool, cut in 2-3 layers.
Fill with coffee-flavoured butter
cream, then reshape.

Spread the top and sides of
the gâteau with a layer of butter
cream, press almonds round the
sides only. Decorate the top of
gâteau by piping on remaining
butter cream, using a rose pipe
(see photograph on previous
page).
Note: as a variation, this cake
can be split in half and filled
with butter cream. After re-
shaping, the top and sides of the
cake are spread with more butter
cream and decorated all over
with shredded almonds. The
top is then dredged with icing
sugar; top edge can be piped
with rosettes of butter cream.

Gâteau aux groseilles

3 egg quantity of genoese pastry
redcurrant jelly
apricot glaze
white fondant icing
frosted redcurrants

8½-inch diameter layer cake tin

Method
Set oven at 350-375°F or Mark
4-5. Grease and flour cake tin.

Turn the genoese mixture into
the tin and bake in pre-set oven
for about 25-30 minutes. When
cool, split the cake in two,
sandwich the halves with redcurrant jelly and then reshape
cake; brush it with apricot
glaze, ice with white fondant
and decorate with frosted red-
currants (see photograph on
previous page).

> **Frosted redcurrants**
> Choose good sprays of
> clean, fresh redcurrants;
> brush them sparingly with
> slightly-beaten egg white
> and dip each spray in caster
> sugar. Leave sprays on a
> sieve or wire rack to dry.

Gâteau Cendrillon

3 oz plain flour
pinch of salt
3 eggs
scant 3¼ oz caster sugar
1 tablespoon coffee essence
1½ oz butter (melted)
coffee-flavoured butter cream
apricot glaze
coffee-flavoured fondant icing
8-10 browned hazelnuts, or split
  almonds

9-inch diameter layer cake tin

Method
Grease and flour the cake tin. Set oven at 350-375°F or Mark 4-5.

Sift the flour with the salt. Break the eggs into a bowl, add the sugar and coffee essence and whisk over gentle heat until the mixture is thick and mousse-like. Remove the bowl from the heat and continue whisking until the mixture is cold. Fold in two-thirds of the flour, then the melted butter and lastly the remaining flour. Turn the mixture quickly into the tin and bake in pre-set oven for 30-35 minutes.

When cake is cool, split it in two and sandwich the halves together with a layer of coffee-flavoured butter cream (reserving some for decoration). Re-shape the cake and brush over the top and sides with a thin coating of hot apricot glaze. When glaze is set, ice cake with coffee-flavoured fondant icing, pipe 8-10 rosettes of butter cream around (one for each portion/slice of cake) and decorate each one with a browned hazelnut (or a split almond).

Gâteau d'ananas
(Pineapple cake)

3 egg quantity of genoese pastry
butter cream (flavoured with
  kirsch, or lemon juice)
apricot glaze
candied pineapple
white fondant icing

8-inch diameter cake tin

Method
Prepare tin by greasing it, lining bottom only with a disc of greaseproof paper, greasing again and dusting first with caster sugar, then with flour.

Set oven at 350°F or Mark 4.

Turn genoese mixture into tin and bake in pre-set oven for about 30 minutes. When cool, split cake in two and sandwich halves with the flavoured butter cream. Reshape cake and brush top and sides with a thin coating of hot apricot glaze, then leave it to set. Arrange slices of candied pineapple over the top of the cake and coat the top and sides with a very thin layer of fondant icing.

Candied pineapple
Take one small can of pineapple slices and divide each slice horizontally, if very thick. Put half the juice from the can into a frying pan with 2 rounded tablespoons of granulated sugar. Allow this to dissolve over slow heat, add the pineapple and cook gently until transparent. Do not allow the sugar to caramelise, and turn the slices from time to time. Use the candied pineapple when cold.

Gâteau au chocolat

2¼ oz plain flour
pinch of salt
2 oz chocolate (unsweetened)
about 2½ fl oz water
3 eggs
4½ oz caster sugar
2 oz plain block chocolate
6 oz butter cream
chocolate caraque
a little icing sugar (to decorate)

9½-inch diameter layer cake tin

Method

Set oven at 350°F or Mark 4. Grease and flour the cake tin.

Sift the flour with the salt. Grate or slice the unsweetened chocolate, melt it in the water over gentle heat to a thick cream, then set it aside to cool.

Whisk the eggs and sugar together in a bowl over a pan of hot water until thick and mousse-like; remove the bowl from the heat and continue whisking until the mixture is cold. Fold the flour into the mixture, then add the melted chocolate. Turn mixture into the tin and bake in pre-set oven for about 35 minutes.

While the cake is cooking, melt the plain chocolate on a plate over a pan of hot water; when it is quite smooth, beat it into the butter cream.

When cake is cool, split it in two and sandwich with a thin layer of the chocolate butter cream. Reshape the cake, spread top and sides with butter cream and press chocolate caraque over and around it, then sprinkle with icing sugar. To get the striped effect, lay strips of greaseproof paper over the cake before sprinkling on icing sugar.

Gâteau praliné

4 egg quantity of genoese pastry
6 oz butter cream
apricot glaze
2 oz praline
2 oz ground almonds (browned)

9½-inch diameter deep cake tin

Method
Set oven at 350°F or Mark 4. Grease tin, line bottom only with a disc of greaseproof paper, grease again, dust with caster sugar, then flour. Turn the genoese mixture into tin and bake in pre-set oven for about 35 minutes.

Pound the praline to a smooth paste and add it to the butter cream.

When the cake is cold, split it in two and sandwich the halves together with a thick layer of butter cream. Reshape cake and brush the top and sides with well-reduced apricot glaze. Cover cake with the ground almonds, pressing them on well with a palette knife.

Gâteau Isigny

4 egg quantity of genoese pastry (flavoured with grated rind ½ lemon)
6 oz butter cream (flavoured with either sieved raspberry purée, or sieved raspberry jam)
white fondant icing

9½-inch diameter cake tin; forcing bag and writing pipe

Isigny is a village in Calvados, Normandy, which is famous throughout France for its butter and cream.

Method
Set oven at 350°F or Mark 4.

Grease tin, line bottom only with a disc of greaseproof paper, grease again, dust with caster sugar, then flour. Turn genoese mixture into tin and bake in pre-set oven for about 35 minutes. When cool, split gâteau in two and fill with a thin layer of the raspberry-flavoured butter cream.

Cover top and sides of gâteau with more butter cream and leave until firm. Ice cake with fondant icing and use a writing pipe to write 'Isigny' on top.

Gâteau flamande

4 oz quantity of French flan
 pastry
2 oz crystallised cherries
2-3 tablespoons kirsch
2 egg quantity of frangipane
 (flavoured with 1 tablespoon
 kirsch)

To decorate
2 oz flaked almonds
4 tablespoons thick glacé icing

8-inch diameter flan ring

Method
Line pastry dough into flan ring
(see page 49). Slice cherries,
reserving a few for decoration,
and macerate in the kirsch. Set
oven at 375°F or Mark 5.

Prepare the frangipane and
flavour with kirsch.

Place the cherries at the
bottom of the flan, cover with
frangipane and place the almonds on top. Bake gâteau in
pre-set oven for about 45
minutes. When cool, brush
gâteau with glacé icing and
decorate with reserved cherries.

Gâteau Alexandra

4¼ oz (125 g) caster sugar
2½ oz (75 g) ground almonds
4 eggs
3½ oz (100 g) plain block chocolate
1 tablespoon water
2¾ oz (80 g) fécule
¾ oz (20 g) plain flour
2½ oz (75 g) butter
apricot glaze
chocolate fondant icing

8-inch square cake tin

Method
Set oven at 350°F or Mark 4. Prepare tin by lining with buttered greaseproof paper.

Place the sugar, ground almonds, 1 whole egg and 3 egg yolks in a basin and beat with a spatula until white and mousse-like (or work in an electric blender). Melt the chocolate with the water in a pan, over gentle heat, until it is a thick cream, then add to egg mixture. Stiffly whisk egg whites. Next fold the two flours and the egg whites into the mixture. Lastly, mix in the butter, which should be warmed until soft and pourable, but great care should be taken not to make it hot and oily.

Place the mixture in the prepared tin and bake in the preset oven for 50-60 minutes, reducing the temperature to 325°F or Mark 3 after the first 30 minutes. When the cake is cold, brush with reduced apricot glaze and ice with chocolate fondant. Leave undecorated.

Gâteau Mercédès

8 oz quantity of French flan pastry

For almond filling
8½ oz (250 g) ground almonds
8½ oz (250 g) caster sugar
4 egg whites
kirsch (to flavour)
2½ oz (75 g) crystallised fruits
3 tablespoons apricot jam
1½-2 oz shredded almonds
apricot glaze

8-inch diameter spring-form tin

Top: lining the tin with French flan pastry for gâteau Mercédès
Above: pouring the almond mixture on top of the fruit in the pastry case

Method

Make French flan pastry dough and chill for 30 minutes.

Set oven at 350°F or Mark 4.

To prepare filling: pound the almonds and sugar with the egg whites and flavour with kirsch. Shred the fruits and moisten them with the jam.

Roll out the chilled pastry dough and line it into the tin; prick the base lightly with a fork and place the fruits on it. Fill the flan with the almond mixture and cover this with the shredded almonds.

Bake in the pre-set oven for about 45 minutes until set and golden-brown. When gâteau is cool, brush with apricot glaze.

Gâteau Alcazar

For French flan pastry
5¼ oz (150 g) plain flour
pinch of salt
2½ oz (75 g) butter
2½ oz (75 g) caster sugar
2 egg yolks

For almond mousse filling
4¼ oz (125 g) ground almonds
4¼ oz (125 g) caster sugar
3 eggs
1-2 drops vanilla essence
2 tablespoons kirsch
2 oz (60 g) butter (melted)

apricot glaze

For decoration
3½ oz (100 g) almonds
3½ oz (100 g) caster sugar
egg white
4 tablespoons apricot jam
6-8 pistachio nuts (halved), or
browned almonds

Deep 8-9 inch diameter sandwich tin, or moule a manque; forcing bag with ¼-inch éclair pipe

Method
Prepare the pastry dough and chill for 1 hour. Set oven at 375°F or Mark 5. Meanwhile, prepare almond mousse filling. Pound the ground almonds with the sugar, add 1 egg, vanilla essence, and kirsch to flavour; work well with a spatula until thick and white. Separate remaining eggs; stiffly whisk whites. Add one yolk after the other to mixture; when it is mousse-like, fold in egg whites, then add the melted butter.

Watchpoint The mixing of the egg white and butter must be done lightly but thoroughly.
Line the sandwich tin, or

Decorating gâteau Alcazar with a piped lattice of almond paste

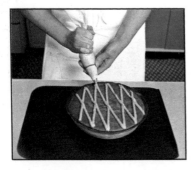

36

moule à manqué, with the pastry dough, cutting it about ¼ inch above the rim. Prick the pastry bottom and coat with a thin layer of apricot glaze. Fill with the almond mousse and cook in pre-set oven for 45 minutes.

While the cake is cooking prepare the almond decoration. Pound the almonds and sugar together and moisten with egg white, adding it a little at a time so that the paste is moist but not liquid (it must hold its shape when piped).

To decorate and finish cake: turn it out and leave to cool, upside down, on a wire rack.

Watchpoint The cake is turned upside down to cool to make sure that the surface of the almond filling is flat before decorating.

Place the almond mixture in a bag fitted with a ¼-inch éclair pipe and pipe the mixture on the top (lattice-fashion). Place in oven at 350°F or Mark 4 for about 10 minutes to colour, but take care not to burn the cake.

Reduce 4 tablespoons of apricot jam, by simmering in a pan until very thick; with a brush, fill each diamond in the lattice pattern with this. Place half a pistachio or almond in each diamond.

Gâteau Pithiviers

8 oz quantity of puff pastry
beaten egg
icing sugar (for dusting)

For almond cream
3½ oz (100 g) ground almonds
3½ oz (100 g) caster sugar
1¼ oz (40 g) butter
2 egg yolks
2-3 drops of vanilla essence, or
liqueur glass of orange flower
water, or rum

This gâteau is a speciality of the town of Pithiviers in the Loire district of France. Like the Mercédès (page 34), it is a rich almond mixture. The recipe given here uses ground almonds, and no doubt this is more convenient for domestic purposes. However, for perfection, use whole, freshly blanched almonds, grate them through a nut mill and pound until perfectly smooth before putting in the butter, sugar and egg. The result is not so 'cakey' and you get a richer almond paste than with ground almonds; the difference is quite noticeable. Up to about 20 years ago ground almonds were not known in France and only whole almonds were used for this type of work.

Method

Set the oven at 400-425°F or Mark 6-7.

First prepare almond cream: blend the ground almonds with the sugar and butter, then work in egg yolks and flavouring until the paste whitens.

Divide the pastry dough into one-third and two-thirds, roll out and cut 2 rounds, 6-7 inches in diameter, making one (the top) twice as thick as the other. Place the thinner round of dough on a slightly dampened baking sheet and spread the centre with the almond cream. Brush the edge of this round with water and place over it the thicker round of dough. Pinch to seal round the edges. Brush the top with beaten egg and decorate with the back of a knife. Bake in pre-set oven for 20-30 minutes. Five minutes before the cooking is complete, dust the top of the cake with icing sugar and return it to the oven to caramelise.

Gâteau nougatine

2 oz (60 g) butter
3½ oz (100 g) plain flour
pinch of salt
4 eggs
4½ oz (135 g) caster sugar
2 oz (60 g) hazelnuts (ground
   and browned)
4 oz (120 g) nougat
butter cream
chocolate fondant icing

9-inch diameter layer cake tin

Method
Brush tin with melted butter or lard, line with greaseproof paper, brush with fat, then dust with flour.

Set oven at 350°F or Mark 4.

Warm the butter very gently to a pourable, but not oily, consistency. Sift flour with the salt. Break the eggs into a bowl, add the sugar and whisk gently over a pan of hot water until the mixture is thick and mousse-like. Remove bowl from the heat and continue whisking until the bowl is cold. Fold in two-thirds of the flour, then the melted butter, prepared nuts and lastly the remaining flour. Turn the mixture at once into the prepared tin and bake in pre-set moderate oven for about 30-35 minutes.

Meanwhile crush the nougat until fine and smooth and add half to the butter cream. When the cake is cool, split it in three and sandwich with thin layers of the flavoured butter cream. Ice the top of cake with chocolate fondant, spread the sides with remaining butter cream and press round crushed nougat. Decorate with crescents of nougat.

Nougat

4-6 oz (150-180 g) caster sugar
4 oz (120 g) almonds (blanched,
   finely chopped and lightly
   toasted in the oven)
1 lemon (oiled)

Method
Dissolve the sugar over very gentle heat, then cook it to a caramel; add the almonds gradually, stirring them in with a metal spoon. Turn the nougat on to an oiled slab or tin and roll with an oiled lemon. Cut nougat while still warm, making some of it into crescents for decoration.

Watchpoint It is important to work quickly once the nougat is cooked. Should it become brittle and difficult, put it in a warm oven for a few minutes.

Gâteau pistache

3 eggs
3¾ oz (105 g) caster sugar
2¾ oz (80 g) plain flour
1 oz (30 g) butter
6 oz butter cream (1)
1 oz (30 g) pistachio nuts
　(blanched and pounded to
　a paste)
apricot glaze
glacé icing (made with 12 oz
　(360 g) icing sugar, sugar syrup
　and 1 tablespoon kirsch)
few whole pistachio nuts (to
　decorate)

*Deep 8-inch diameter cake tin, or
moule à manqué*

Method

Set oven at 350°F or Mark 4.
Prepare tin as for gâteau aux
noisettes (see right).

Put the eggs into a basin with
the sugar; whisk over a pan of
hot water until the mixture is
white and thick. Fold flour into
the mixture with a metal spoon,
then the well softened butter.
Turn the mixture into tin and
bake in pre-set oven for 30-35
minutes, or until the cake comes
away from the side of the tin.
Turn it out on to a rack to cool.

Flavour butter cream with the
pistachio paste.

Split cake in two, sandwich
halves with butter cream. Brush
the cake with warm apricot
glaze. To make the glacé icing,
sift the icing sugar and work in
enough of the syrup to make a
thick cream. Add the kirsch and
warm to just above blood heat
(100°F). Ice the cake and
decorate it with the whole
pistachio nuts.

Gâteau progrès

5 egg whites
7 oz (200 g) caster sugar
5½ oz (160 g) ground almonds
2-3 drops of vanilla essence
6 oz butter cream
4 oz (120 g) plain block chocolate
2 oz (60 g) praline

To finish
finely chopped almonds
　(browned)
icing sugar

Method

First grease and flour 5 baking
sheets. Set oven at 350°F or
Mark 4.

Whisk egg whites until stiff
but not dry and fold into the
sugar, ground almonds and
vanilla essence. Spread the
mixture on the baking sheets to
give 5 rounds, 7½-8 inches in
diameter. Bake in a pre-set
moderate oven for about 10
minutes. Trim rounds, while
still hot, with a sharp knife, then
put them on a wire rack to cool.
Note: these rounds may be
baked in rotation, greasing and
flouring sheets between baking.

Cut the chocolate into small
pieces and put it on a plate
over a pan of hot water to melt
—do not allow it to become hot
—then add it to the butter cream.
Put 1 rounded tablespoon of
chocolate butter cream aside
for decoration, crush praline
to a smooth paste and add it
to the remainder.

Sandwich the meringue rounds
with the butter cream and
spread the top and sides with
it; press the browned almonds
around. Dredge the top with
icing sugar and pipe 'Progrès'
with the reserved butter cream.

Gâteau aux noisettes

4 oz (120 g) hazelnuts
2½ oz (75 g) plain flour
pinch of salt
1½ oz (45 g) butter
4 eggs (separated)
4½ oz (135 g) caster sugar
butter cream
2-3 tablespoons kirsch, or
   coffee essence (optional)
white fondant icing

*9-inch diameter layer cake tin; forcing
  bag and 8-cut vegetable rose pipe*

Method

Set oven at 375°F or Mark 5. Brush the tin with melted butter or lard, line with greaseproof paper, brush with fat, then dust with flour.

Brown the nuts, reserve 1 oz (30 g) and pound the rest, or put them through a nut mill, until smooth. Divide the ground nuts in two portions. Sift the flour with the salt and set it on one side.

Warm the butter until soft and pourable. Place the egg yolks and sugar in a bowl and work together with a wooden spoon until white and creamy. Now, using a metal spoon, fold in one portion of the ground and browned nuts. Whisk the egg whites until stiff and fold them into the mixture alternately with the sifted flour. Lastly add the melted butter. Turn the mixture at once into the prepared tin and bake in a pre-set moderate oven for about 45 minutes.

Mix the remaining ground nuts into the butter cream and flavour, if wished, with kirsch or coffee essence. When the cake is cold, split it in two and sandwich the halves with a layer of butter cream. Coat the top of the cake with white fondant icing and spread the sides with butter cream. Keep about 14 of the reserved browned nuts whole and chop the remainder into rough pieces and press them round the sides of the cake. Finish the top edge of the cake with rosettes of remaining butter cream. Place a whole nut between each rosette.

Doboz torte

5 oz (150 g) plain flour
pinch of salt
4 eggs
6 oz (180 g) caster sugar
8 oz butter cream (flavoured with
 4 oz (120 g) plain block
 chocolate)

For caramel
5 oz (150 g) lump sugar
¼ pint water

To finish
crushed caramel, or grated
 chocolate
chocolate butter cream (for
 rosettes)

This cake is of Austrian origin.

*Marking the caramelised round of
Doboz torte into portions for cutting*

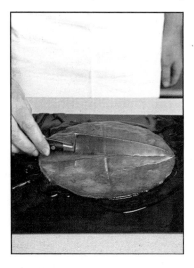

Method

Prepare 6 baking sheets by brushing them with melted lard or oil and dusting lightly with flour; then mark an 8-inch circle on each one, using a plate or pan lid as a guide. Set the oven at 375°F or Mark 5.

Sift the flour with the salt. Break the eggs in a bowl, add the sugar. Place bowl over pan of hot water on gentle heat and whisk mixture until it is thick and white. Remove bowl from the heat and continue whisking until it is cold. Lightly fold the flour into the mixture, using a metal spoon. Divide mixture into 6 portions and spread each over a circle on the prepared sheets (this can be done by using fewer sheets in rotation, but each time the baking sheet to be re-used must be wiped, re-greased and floured). Bake in a pre-set moderate oven for about 5-6 minutes.

Trim each round with a sharp knife while still on the baking sheet, then lift on to a wire rack to cool. Take 1 round, lay it on an oiled sheet ready to coat with the caramel.

To prepare caramel: melt the sugar in the water over a very low heat without boiling. When completely dissolved, increase the heat and cook it rapidly to a rich brown caramel. Pour this at once over the single cake round and, when caramel is just about set, mark it into portions with an oiled knife and trim edges.

Sandwich the six rounds together with chocolate butter cream, putting the caramel-covered round on top. Spread the sides with more butter cream

and press round crushed caramel or grated chocolate. Pipe
a rosette of butter cream on
each portion.

*Doboz torte is decorated with
crushed caramel and rosettes of
chocolate-flavoured butter cream*

Gâteau mille feuilles au citron

8 oz quantity of puff pastry
¾ pint double cream
5½ oz apricot glaze

For lemon curd
8 oz caster sugar
4 oz unsalted butter
grated rind and juice of 2 large
    lemons
3 eggs (well beaten)

For decoration
small shapes made from
    trimmings of puff pastry
crystallised fruits
almonds, or pistachio nuts

4-5 inch diameter plain cutter

You will need a third of this quantity of lemon curd for gâteau mille feuilles au citron. Pour remainder into a warm, dry jar, cover tightly and store in a cool, dry place.

Method

Set oven at 400°F or Mark 6, and dampen a baking sheet.

Roll out pastry dough very thinly and cut 2 rounds the size of a dessert plate; remove the centres of each round with the cutter to leave a large ring of pastry. From remaining dough cut 1 plain circle, a little thicker and larger than the rings, to form a base for the cake.

Place the pastry rings on the baking sheet, prick them well with a fork and bake in pre-set hot oven for 8 minutes. Then prick and bake the circle on a dampened baking sheet for 12-15 minutes. Make trimmings into stars, diamonds, etc., bake in hot oven for 5-7 minutes until brown, then leave to cool.

Put all the ingredients for

Gâteau mille feuilles is decorated with small pastry shapes, crystallised fruit and cream

lemon curd into an enamel pan or stone jam jar, standing in boiling water. Stir gently over low heat until mixture is thick. (It must not boil or it will curdle.) Pour into a bowl and allow to cool.

When all the pastry is cool, brush with warm apricot glaze and mount one ring on top of another on the base. Brush the top and sides of gâteau with apricot glaze and decorate with the small pastry shapes, crystallised fruit or chopped nuts.

To serve: reserve a little cream for decoration and whip the remainder until it begins to thicken, then fold in the lemon curd. Fill the gâteau and decorate the top with rosettes of whipped cream, crystallised fruit and chopped nuts.

Gâteau à l'orange

4¼ oz (125 g) caster sugar
zest, or finely grated rind, of
  1 orange
4 egg yolks
1-2 drops of carmine (optional)
1¾ oz (50 g) plain flour
1¾ oz (50 g) arrowroot
3 egg whites

To finish
apricot glaze
orange fondant, or glacé, icing
candied orange peel (cut into
  diamonds, or crescents)

Deep 8-inch diameter sandwich tin, or moule à manqué

Method
Well grease and flour the tin or moule à manqué. Set oven at 325-350°F or Mark 3-4.

Put the sugar in a basin with the orange zest or rind and work together well, adding egg yolks one at a time. Continue to beat mixture with a wooden spoon until it is creamy and white. At this stage add the carmine to colour it a very light pink. Stir in the flour and arrowroot, well sifted together. Whip egg whites and cut and fold into the mixture. Be careful not to over-mix but keep the light and fluffy consistency. Tip into prepared tin or a moule à manqué and bake in a very moderate oven, pre-set, for 35-40 minutes. Take out cake and leave to cool for a few minutes.

Turn cake out and brush it lightly with an apricot glaze. When cold, ice and decorate with candied orange peel.

Gâteau d'Amatio

For almond pastry
6 oz (170 g) plain flour
2½ oz (75 g) ground almonds
3 oz (90 g) butter
3 oz (90 g) caster sugar
2 egg yolks
grated rind of ½ lemon

For pastry cream
¾ oz (20 g) plain flour
½ oz (15 g) cornflour
2 oz (60 g) caster sugar
2 egg yolks
½ pint milk
vanilla pod
1 egg white
praline

To finish
1 egg white (lightly beaten)
sugar (for dusting)

7-8 inch diameter flan ring

Method

To prepare pastry: sift flour on to a pastry board or marble slab. Make well in the centre, in it place the remaining ingredients and work them up quickly to a paste. Chill for 30 minutes before rolling out. Set oven at 350°F or Mark 4.

Now prepare pastry cream: sift flours into a bowl, add sugar and egg yolks. Cream well together, adding a little cold milk if necessary. Heat remaining milk with vanilla pod, strain it on to egg mixture, blend and return to the pan. Stir over medium heat (or use a double saucepan). When on the boil, whip the egg white stiffly, turn a little of the cream into a bowl and fold in the white by degrees. Then return this to the pan. Stir carefully for a few minutes over the heat, then turn into a bowl to cool. Add a coffee cup of praline to pastry cream.

Roll out two-thirds of the pastry dough and line into a flan ring. Fill with the praline cream, roll out the remaining dough and cover the flan ring. Brush with egg white, dust with sugar and bake in pre-set moderate oven for 40 minutes.

Pâtisseries

Real French pâtisseries are among the most tempting of foods. Few people can pass the window of a high class pastry shop without stopping to gaze longingly through the window, and having got so far it's but a short fall to the interior and counter.

With a little care and patience you can make these delicious concoctions yourself, and be sure of delighting even the most fastidious guests. You will find them asking you the name of your pâtissier, and they will hardly believe you when you say you make them yourself.

As with the large gâteaux, these small cakes follow tradition strictly where names and decorations are concerned, and any deviation is frowned upon.

Certain foundations are basic to many pâtisseries, with French flan pastry and genoese occurring most frequently; puff pastry is also extremely useful for producing such cream-filled delights as mille feuilles and cream horns, and choux gives a small range of delicacies all its own.

A 4 oz quantity of French flan pastry will line 9-12 boat shaped moulds or tartlet tins (see page 48). In many of our recipes we have not given any specific quantity of pastry, as it is more usual to make up a quantity of the basic foundation and bake a selection of cakes with different fillings. Or, if you have been making larger gâteaux you can use up the trimmings for small pâtisseries.

Moulds

Some pâtisseries and gâteaux are made in special moulds or tins. The French tartlet mould is best for French flan pastry. It is fairly deep, measures from 2-2½ inches in diameter and is obtainable from any good kitchen ironmonger.

A boat mould can also be used for French flan pastry. Here a medium-size mould, eg. 2½-3 inches long, is best, especially one with a slightly wide base, rather than one that is too long and narrow.

Moule à manqué

This is similar to a deep sandwich tin, has sloping sides and is usually plain, although some have a classic pattern on the bottom. They are used for genoese, sponges and other cakes, especially those to be iced. For icing, the cake is inverted so that icing runs down the sloping sides.

Mixtures to be served plain, such as frangipane, and cream sweets look attractive in these moulds.

They are obtainable in London from Divertimenti, 68-70 Marylebone Lane, W1 and Leon Jaeggi, 232 Tottenham Court Road, W1, and at kitchenware shops around the country.

A variety of moulds: from top left, moule à manqués, brioches, a six-madeleine tray, tartlet and boat moulds in two sizes

Lining French flan pastry into moulds

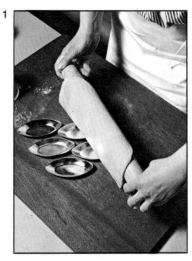

1 *Using a rolling pin to lay the dough over the boat moulds*
2 *Pressing dough into moulds with a floured ball of dough*
3 *Rolling off dough edges, first one way, then the other*

Tartlet moulds. Take half the given dough and roll it out very thinly. Set 4-5 moulds on your work surface. Lift up dough on rolling pin and lay over the moulds. Cut off a small piece, roll it into a small ball (about the size of a marble). Dip this ball lightly into flour and use it to pat and press the dough into the moulds, easing it gently in. When moulds are well lined, roll off the edges with the rolling pin, first one way, then the other.

Add the trimmings to remaining dough and line remaining moulds in the same way.

Flan ring. Roll out pastry dough ¼ inch thick. Place the flan ring on a baking sheet and proceed as for tartlet moulds.

Lisettes

3-4 oz quantity of French flan
  pastry
apricot jam
2 egg whites
2 oz caster sugar
2 oz ground almonds
candied orange peel
icing sugar

*Approximately 12 boat moulds (with
  fluted edges)*

Method
Set the oven at 350-375°F or
Mark 4-5.

Roll out the pastry dough very
thinly and line it into the moulds.
Prick the bottoms with a fork
and put half a teaspoon of apricot jam into each one.

Whisk the egg whites until
stiff and dry, then fold in the
sugar and almonds. Fill each
pastry case with this mixture,
put a 'diamond' of the candied
orange peel in the middle of
each one, dust them with icing
sugar and bake in pre-set oven
for 10-12 minutes.

Gâteaux St. André

4 oz quantity of French flan
  pastry
apple marmelade (made from
  1 lb cooking apples)

For royal icing
5 oz icing sugar
1 egg white
pinch of flour

12 boat moulds

Method
Set oven at 375°F or Mark 5.

Line the moulds with pastry
dough and fill with the apple
marmelade (well reduced and
very cold). Reserve the pastry
scraps to decorate.

To make royal icing: sift the
icing sugar. Whisk the egg
white until frothy, then add to
the icing sugar, 1 tablespoon at
a time, beating well between
each addition. Add the flour.
Continue beating until the mixture will stand in peaks. Cover
the apple marmelade with the
royal icing and place two bands
of pastry, ¼ inch wide, on the
tops to form a St. Andrew's
cross. Bake in the pre-set oven
for about 10 minutes. (See
photograph of finished cakes
on page 52.)

Tartelettes amandines

4 oz quantity of French flan
   pastry
1 egg quantity of frangipane
2 oz almonds (flaked)
apricot, or redcurrant, glaze
2 tablespoons ground almonds
   (for decoration)

12 tartlet moulds

Method

Set oven at 375°F or Mark 5.
   Line moulds with pastry
dough, prick bottoms with a
fork and fill each case with
frangipane. Scatter the flaked
almonds over the tops and bake
for 12-15 minutes in pre-set
oven. As soon as the tartlets are
cooked, remove them from the
moulds, brush the tops with
hot glaze and decorate the outside edges with a thin line of
ground almonds.
Note: it is quicker and easier
to fill the tartlet moulds if the
frangipane is put into a piping
bag fitted with a plain pipe.
(See photograph of finished
cakes on page 52.)

Bateaux de miel

4 oz quantity of French flan
   pastry

For filling
3 oz butter (unsalted)
3 oz caster sugar
3 oz ground almonds
1 tablespoon honey
coffee essence (to taste)
coffee fondant icing

12-16 boat moulds

Method

Set oven at 375°F or Mark 5.
   Line the moulds with pastry
dough and bake blind in pre-
set oven for 5-7 minutes, then
remove and leave to cool.
   Meanwhile cream the butter
and sugar together until light,
stir in the ground almonds and
honey and flavour with the
coffee essence to taste. When
pastry cases are cold, fill with
the coffee almond cream, doming it well and shaping it with a
small, sharp knife. Leave filled
cases in a cool place to set,
then ice with the coffee
fondant and leave undecorated.
(See photograph of finished
cakes on page 52.)

Madeleines

2 oz plain flour
2 eggs
2 oz caster sugar
2 oz butter

12-18 madeleine moulds

These are traditional French madeleines, shaped like shallow, oval shells with fluted tops.

Method

Butter and flour the tins and set oven at 375°F or Mark 5.

Sift the flour. Warm the butter gently until it is just soft and pourable, taking great care not to make it hot or oily. Place the eggs and sugar in a basin and whisk together until thick and mousse-like *(not* over hot water), then fold in the sifted flour and the softened butter.

Fill the tins with the mixture and bake in pre-set oven for about 10 minutes.

Bateaux Célestins

4 oz quantity of French flan
   pastry
2 tablespoons apricot jam
½ quantity of madeleine mixture
   (left)
rind of 1 orange (grated)
apricot glaze
orange glacé, or fondant, icing

12-16 boat moulds

Method

Set oven at 375°F or Mark 5.

Line moulds with pastry dough. Place a little apricot jam at the bottom of each case, then fill each one with the madeleine mixture flavoured with grated orange rind. Bake cakes in pre-set oven for about 10 minutes, then turn moulds upside down on to a rack to cool.

Brush the tops with hot apricot glaze and, when set, coat top of each cake with an orange glacé or fondant icing.

Chocolatines

2 egg quantity of genoese
  pastry
6 oz butter cream 1, flavoured
  with 4 oz melted chocolate
finely-chopped browned, or
  ground, almonds

6-inch square cake tin

Method
Prepare tin by greasing it, lining bottom only with a disc of
greaseproof paper, greasing
again and dusting first with
caster sugar, then with flour.
Set oven at 350°F or Mark 4.
  Fill genoese into tin and bake
for about 30-35 minutes. When
cool, split and sandwich with
a thin layer of chocolate butter
cream. Reshape the cake, trim
and cut into 2-inch squares.
Spread the top and sides of each
square with the butter cream
and press the almonds round
the sides only. Decorate tops
with rosettes of the same chocolate flavoured butter cream.

Mokatines

2 egg quantity of genoese
  pastry
3 oz coffee-flavoured butter
  cream 1
apricot glaze
8 oz coffee-flavoured fondant
  icing

6-inch square cake tin

Method
Bake the genoese in the prepared tin (see left) and, when
cool, split and sandwich with a
thin layer of coffee butter cream.
Reshape the cake, trim and
cut into neat oblongs 2½ inches
long and 1 inch wide. Brush
the top and sides with hot
apricot glaze, ice with the
fondant icing and decorate
with a piping of the coffee
butter cream.
Note: as a variation this cake
can be cut into small rounds.
Split these and fill with a thin
layer of coffee butter cream.
Reshape and spread the top
and sides with butter cream,
roll in chopped browned almonds, and pipe a small rosette
of coffee butter cream in the
centre.

*Selection of pâtisseries: from left
to right, chocolatines, madeleines,
tartelettes amandines, bateaux de
miel, mirlitons, bateaux de miel,
tartelettes amandines, gâteaux St.
André*

Printaniers

**2 egg quantity of genoese
  pastry**
8 oz butter cream 2
vanilla essence
coffee essence
a little sieved strawberry jam
**carmine, or cochineal (for
  colouring)**
8 oz quantity of fondant icing

*Swiss roll tin, or paper case, 12
inches by 8 inches; forcing bag
and 5/8-inch plain pipe*

Method
Set oven at 350°F or Mark 4.
Prepare genoese and bake in
a greased and floured swiss roll
tin or paper case for 25-30
minutes. When cool, split cake
and sandwich halves with a little
vanilla-flavoured butter cream.
Trim the cake and cut it into
long strips, 1½ inches wide.

Divide remaining butter cream
into three portions; flavour
one with vanilla, another with
coffee and the last portion
with strawberry jam (adding a
few drops of carmine, to colour
it a delicate pink).

Fill forcing bag and pipe on
the top three lines of butter
cream; first the vanilla and
coffee, side by side, then the
strawberry on the top. Place
cakes in a refrigerator to harden
butter cream. Then coat with
white fondant icing and, when
set, cut diagonally into sections
about ¾ inch wide.

To make a paper case

To make a paper case, take a
piece of thick greaseproof paper
or non-stick (silicone) kitchen
paper 1-2 inches larger than the
size you require, for example
14 inches by 10 inches. Fold
over the ends and sides to form
a border of about 1½ inches. Cut
a slit at each corner and fold one
cut piece over the other to mitre
the corner. Fasten each corner
with a paper clip so the borders
stand up. Slide case on to a
baking sheet.

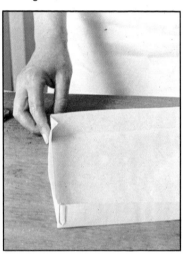

*Secure corners with paper clips
and slide case on to a baking sheet.
Lightly brush greaseproof paper
with oil or melted butter before use*

Florettes

4 oz quantity of French flan
   pastry
2 tablespoons apricot jam

For filling
2 small egg whites
3 oz icing sugar (sifted)
2½ oz ground almonds
kirsch, or 2 drops of almond
   essence (to flavour)

To finish
2 tablespoons almonds (blanched
   and roughly chopped)
icing sugar

10-12 tartlet moulds

Method
Set oven at 375°F or Mark 5.
   Line the moulds with the
pastry dough, prick the bottoms
with a fork, then place a little
apricot jam on the bottom of
each one.
   To prepare the filling: whisk
the egg whites until stiff, fold
in the icing sugar and ground
almonds and flavour with kirsch
or almond essence. Divide this
mixture between the tartlet
moulds. Decorate the tops with
the roughly chopped almonds,
dredge with icing sugar and
bake in pre-set oven for about
15 minutes.

Mirlitons

4 oz quantity of French flan
   pastry
2 tablespoons apricot jam

For filling
4 macaroons (see page 82)
2 eggs
3½ oz caster sugar
2-3 drops of vanilla essence

To decorate
halved blanched almonds
icing sugar

10-12 tartlet moulds

Mirlitons are a speciality of the
French town of Rouen.

Method
Set oven at 300°F or Mark 2.
   Line the moulds, prick the
pastry bottoms with a fork and
place a little apricot jam at the
bottom of each one.
   Break the macaroons in small
pieces and bake in pre-set oven
for about 10-15 minutes, or
until quite dry, then crush them
with a rolling pin and put
through a sieve.
   Increase the oven heat to
350°F or Mark 4.
   Whip the eggs and sugar together until very thick and
mousse-like, add the sieved
macaroons and flavour with
vanilla essence. Fill the mixture
into the moulds, decorate each
top with three almond halves,
dredge with icing sugar and
bake in pre-set oven for about
15 minutes.

Fanchonettes à la vanille

4 oz quantity of French flan
   pastry
½ quantity of pastry cream
   recipe (vanilla-flavoured)

For meringue
2 egg whites
4 oz caster sugar

To finish
1 tablespoon redcurrant jelly
icing sugar

*Approximately 10 tartlet moulds;
   forcing bag and ¼-inch plain pipe*

Method
Set oven at 350°F or Mark 4.
   Line the moulds with pastry
dough, prick the bottoms with
a fork, fill with pastry cream
and bake in the pre-set oven
for 10-12 minutes.
   To make the meringue: whisk
egg whites until quite stiff, then
whisk in 1 dessertspoon of the
sugar and fold the remainder in
with a metal spoon.
   When the tartlets are cooked
cover them with a layer of
meringue. Put the rest of the
meringue in forcing bag. Pipe
a circle of meringue in the
centre of each tartlet, then
decorate the outside edge with
small rounds of meringue. Dust
tops with icing sugar, turn the
oven down to 300°F or Mark 2
and cook until meringue is set
and biscuit-coloured (about 15
minutes).
   When the tartlets are cool,
decorate the centre with a
little redcurrant jelly and dust
with icing sugar.

Bateaux bruxellois

4 oz quantity of French flan
   pastry
½ quantity of pastry cream
   recipe
2 oz ground almonds

For decoration
6 glacé cherries
strip of angelica (cut into
   24 diamonds)
icing sugar

Approximately 12 boat moulds

Method
Set oven at 375°F or Mark 5.
   Line moulds with pastry
dough and prick bottoms. Mix
the pastry cream with the ground
almonds and fill into the moulds.
Decorate each one with a half
cherry and two diamonds of
angelica. Dust with icing sugar
and bake in pre-set oven for
10-12 minutes.

Croissants de Provence

4 oz ground almonds
4 oz caster sugar
1 tablespoon apricot glaze (very thick)
vanilla essence
1 large egg white
little plain flour
1 egg (beaten)
2 oz almonds (blanched and chopped)

To finish
1 tablespoon granulated sugar (dissolved in 2 tablespoons milk)

Method

Set oven at 350°F or Mark 4. Pound the ground almonds well, adding the sugar gradually. Then mix in the apricot glaze and vanilla essence, adding the egg white a little at a time and only sufficient to make a paste that can be rolled in the hand.

Divide the mixture into pieces the size of a large walnut or golf ball and roll them, with a little flour, to the size and shape of your finger. Brush these finger shapes with beaten egg and then roll them in the chopped nuts (making sure that the croissants are well covered).

Bend the shapes into croissants, place on greaseproof paper, brush with egg and bake in a pre-set oven for 10 minutes. When they are cooked and still hot, brush them lightly with sweetened milk.

Tom Pouce
(Tom Thumb)

4 oz quantity of French flan pastry

For filling
2¾ oz butter
2¾ oz caster sugar
2¾ oz ground almonds
1-2 tablespoons sugar syrup
coffee essence
8 oz coffee-flavoured fondant, or glacé, icing
6 almonds (browned and split)

Method

Set oven at 375°F or Mark 5. Roll out pastry dough and cut into 24 small squares. Bake in pre-set oven for 8-10 minutes, then leave to cool.

Meanwhile prepare the filling: cream the butter, add the sugar, beat well until light, then work in the ground almonds and enough sugar syrup to make a soft consistency. Flavour this with coffee essence to taste.

Ice 12 of the squares with the coffee-flavoured icing and decorate with a half almond.

Pipe the coffee-almond filling on to the other 12 squares, then place the iced squares on top.

Fourées au miel

(Small honey biscuits)

4 oz quantity, or trimmings, of
    French flan pastry
3 oz glacé, or crystallised, fruit
1 tablespoon rum
a little thick honey
icing sugar (for dusting)

This quantity makes approximately 9 small honey biscuits.

Method

Set oven at 375°F or Mark 5;
grease the baking sheets. Chop
the fruits finely and leave them
to soak in the rum for 30 minutes. Mix the fruit into the
French flan pastry dough. Chill
well. Roll it out fairly thinly and
cut into rounds 2 inches in
diameter. Place rounds on baking sheets and bake in pre-set
oven for 10-12 minutes. When
cool, sandwich together in pairs
with a little honey and dust the
tops with icing sugar.

Financières

2½ oz butter
2 oz ground almonds
2 oz caster sugar
scant oz potato flour, or fécule
1 egg
1¾ oz mixed glacé fruits (chopped
    and macerated in rum)
apricot glaze
fondant icing (flavoured with
    rum)
6 glacé cherries

12 boat moulds

Method

Set oven at 350°F or Mark 4.
Cream the butter, add almonds,
sugar, potato flour and egg.
Add the macerated glacé fruit
to the mixture. Grease and flour
the moulds and fill with the
mixture. Bake for 7-10 minutes
in the pre-set oven. Turn out
and cool. Brush the tops with
apricot glaze, then coat with
fondant icing. Place a half
cherry on each.

Tartelettes Sappho

French flan pastry
frangipane
butter cream
praline
white fondant icing
chocolate fondant icing

Boat moulds

Method
Line boat-shaped moulds with French flan pastry dough, fill with frangipane and bake in oven at 350°F or Mark 4.

Reserving a little butter cream for decoration, mix the remainder with a little praline (sieved and pounded until smooth). When tartlets are cold, cover the top with praline butter cream arranged in a dome shape. When it is set, ice with fondant icing, half white, half chocolate, and decorate with a small rosette of the reserved butter cream.

Tartelettes perlées

French flan pastry
almond cream (see gâteau
  Pithiviers, page 38)
icing sugar
apricot glaze
Italian meringue

Forcing bag and writing pipe; deep tartlet tins

Method
Line tins with the pastry dough, prick well and fill with almond cream; dust with icing sugar and bake in oven at 325°F or Mark 3 for 8-10 minutes. When cool, brush cakes with apricot glaze and pipe on a very fine lattice pattern of Italian meringue and then small rounds around the edge (like pearls, hence its name). Dry meringue in the oven for about 2 minutes.

(See photograph of finished tartlets on page 61.)

Italian meringue

2 egg whites
4 oz (120 g) lump sugar
2½ fl oz water

Sugar thermometer

Method
Put the sugar and water in a saucepan and cook quickly to 260°F. Beat the whites stiffly and when sugar syrup is ready add it to the whites, mixing quickly with a whisk, and continue to mix until all the syrup has been absorbed.

Barquettes italiennes

French flan pastry
frangipane
Italian meringue (see page 59)
icing sugar
apricot glaze

Boat moulds; forcing bag and ¼-inch plain pipe

Method

Set oven at 375°F or Mark 5. Line boat-shaped moulds with pastry dough, prick and fill moulds with frangipane. Bake in pre-set oven for about 10 minutes. Turn the boats upside down on a wire rack to cool. Reduce oven to 325-350°F or Mark 3-4. Then turn boats up again and cover the tops with Italian meringue, shaping it to an inverted V with a palette knife.

Put a little of the meringue into a forcing bag and decorate the top of the cakes with a scroll. Dust with icing sugar and place the boats in pre-set oven for 3-5 minutes to set. The cakes should be tinged golden-brown when ready.

Fill a small cornet of grease-proof paper with apricot glaze and pipe a thin line of glaze on top of the meringue scroll.

Basic foundation for petits japonais and petits progrès

1 lb (480 g) caster sugar
8 oz (240 g) ground almonds
8 egg whites

Forcing bag and ¼-inch plain pipe

This quantity will make 8-10 of each type.

Method

Set oven at 275°F or Mark 2. Sift the sugar and almonds together. Beat the whites very stiffly. Fold in the almonds and sugar. Place the mixture in a forcing bag. Pipe out in spirals 2 inches in diameter on a baking sheet lined with non-stick kitchen paper. Cook in oven 45-60 minutes. When cooked, remove from paper and allow to cool.

Petits japonais

basic foundation
vanilla butter cream
white praline

Method

For each cake, take two rings of the basic foundation (cooked and cooled) and sandwich them with a little vanilla butter cream; spread top and sides with the same cream. Cover with white praline and score the top with a knife.

Petits progrès

basic foundation
praline butter cream
crushed praline
melted chocolate

Method

For each cake, take two rings of the basic foundation (cooked and cooled) and sandwich them together with a little praline-flavoured butter cream. Spread the top and sides with the same cream. Cover completely with crushed praline and pipe on the top a small ring (or button) of melted chocolate.

From left to right: tartelettes perlées, barquettes italiennes, duchesses pralinées and petits japonais

Bateaux espagnols

French flan pastry
apricot purée (made with fresh, or dried, fruit)
Italian meringue
grated lemon rind
almonds (finely chopped and browned)

Boat moulds

Method

Set oven at 375°F or Mark 5. Line boat-shaped moulds with pastry dough and bake blind in pre-set oven for 5-7 minutes. When cool, fill moulds with the apricot purée. Add lemon rind to the prepared meringue and pile onto the purée. Dome the meringue well and scatter the chopped almonds over, then colour it quickly in oven at 350°F or Mark 4 for 2-3 minutes.

Duchesses pralinées

For biscuits

3 egg whites
3½ oz (100 g) caster sugar
1 oz (30 g) plain flour
1 oz (30 g) ground almonds
1 oz (30 g) ground hazelnuts (grilled)
1 oz (30 g) butter (melted)

For filling

4 oz coffee-flavoured butter cream

Method

Set oven at 275-325°F or Mark 2-3. Whip egg whites stiffly, fold in the sugar, flour, nuts and the melted butter. Spread biscuit out in ovals on a buttered and floured baking sheet, bake in pre-set oven until golden-brown. Lift ovals off on to a wire rack and when cool sandwich with butter cream.

Masillons

French flan pastry
icing sugar (for dusting)

For almond mixture

5¼ oz (155 g) caster sugar
3½ oz (100 g) ground almonds
2-3 drops of vanilla essence
2 eggs
1 egg white (stiffly whisked)

For topping

½ egg white
2¾ oz (80 g) icing sugar
1¼ oz (35 g) almonds (blanched and finely chopped)

6-8 tartlet moulds

Method

First prepare topping: mix egg white, icing sugar and almonds together until a smooth paste. Set aside. Set oven at 375°F or Mark 5.

Pound the sugar with the almonds and vanilla essence, add the eggs one after the other, and lastly egg white.

Line tartlet moulds with pastry dough, fill with the almond mixture and bake in pre-set oven for about 10 minutes. When tartlets are cooked to a golden-brown, cover with almond paste topping. Dust with icing sugar and place them for a few minutes in the oven, set at 325°F or Mark 3.

Mille feuilles

6 oz puff pastry, or trimmings
½ pint double cream
3 tablespoons raspberry jam

For icing

4-6 oz icing sugar
1½ tablespoons water, or 2 of
 sugar syrup (made with
 2 tablespoons granulated sugar
 dissolved in 4 tablespoons
 water, then boiled for 10 minutes)
2-3 drops of vanilla essence

Spreading the layers of pastry with raspberry jam and whipped cream

Method

Set oven at 425°F or Mark 7.

Roll out prepared pastry dough as thinly as possible to a large rectangle. Lay this over a dampened baking sheet, allowing pastry to come slightly over the edge. Prick well all over with a fork and chill for 5-10 minutes. Then bake in pre-set oven for 10-15 minutes.

When brown in colour, slip a palette knife under pastry and turn it over. Cook in oven for a further 5 minutes, then transfer to a rack to cool. When cold, trim round edges and cut into 3 strips about 3 inches wide. Crush trimmings lightly.

Whip cream, but not too stiffly. Spread one strip of pastry with half the jam, then half the cream. Lay a second strip on top and press down lightly. Spread with rest of jam and cream, top with last strip, press down again.

To make icing: mix icing sugar to a cream with water or sugar syrup, add vanilla essence. Warm icing slightly and use to coat the top. Press trimmings round edges to decorate. (See photograph on page 65.)

Watchpoint Mille feuilles pastry must be well-baked, almost nut-brown in colour. You press layers together to prevent them moving when sliced.

63

Sacristans

6 oz puff pastry, or trimmings
1 egg (beaten)
chopped almonds
icing sugar (for dusting)

Method

Set oven at 425°F or Mark 7.
Roll out pastry dough to a thin
strip, 5 inches wide. Brush with
beaten egg, leaving a border
of about ½ inch at each side.
Sprinkle with almonds and dust
with sifted icing sugar.

Cut into strips about ¾ inch
wide; take up these strips and
twist several times before laying
them on a dampened baking
sheet. Press down each end
firmly. Bake in pre-set oven for
8-10 minutes. Carefully lift
biscuits off baking sheet and
leave to cool on a wire rack.

Cream horns

8 oz rough puff pastry (well
   chilled)
1 egg white (beaten)
strawberry, or raspberry, jam
¼ pint Chantilly cream
pistachio nuts (finely chopped)
   —for decoration

12 cream horn moulds

Method

Lightly grease the moulds and a
baking sheet. Set the oven at
425°F or Mark 7.

Roll out the pastry dough ⅛
inch thick, cut into long, 1 inch
wide strips and brush these with
a very little beaten egg white.
Wind the dough round the
cream horn moulds, starting at
the point and overlapping each
round. Trim the tops, brush
again with egg white, set on a
lightly-greased baking tray and
cook in pre-set oven for 7-8
minutes until crisp and pale
golden-brown.

Remove the horns from the
tins. When cold, put a ½ teaspoon of jam at the bottom of
each horn and fill with Chantilly
cream. Decorate the top of each
one with a small pinch of
pistachio nuts.

Chantilly cream

Whip a ¼-pint carton of double
cream until just thickening;
then add 1 teaspoon caster
sugar and 2-3 drops of vanilla
essence. Then continue beating
until the cream holds its shape.
(In warm weather and in a
warm kitchen, if the sugar and
essence are added before first
whisking, it prevents cream
getting thick.)

Sacristans and mille feuilles (see recipe on page 63) are both made with puff pastry—a good way to use up trimmings left over from other recipes

Palmiers

6 oz puff pastry, or trimmings
caster sugar

Method
Roll out pastry dough to a strip. Dredge well with caster sugar, fold in three and roll out again. Dust once more with sugar, fold in three and roll out. Fold in three again and chill for 15 minutes.

Set oven at 425°F or Mark 7.

Roll out dough to a 10-inch square, about a ¼ inch thick. Fold the edge nearest to you twice over to reach the centre of pastry; repeat this from the other side. Press lightly with rolling pin, then fold in half.

Press again, then with a sharp knife cut across into slices about ½ inch wide. Lay these, cut side down, on a dampened baking sheet, leaving room for them to spread. Open slices slightly, and flatten with the heel of the hand (see shape opposite). Bake in pre-set oven for 10-12 minutes.

When beginning to go brown, turn them over so that both sides will caramelise. When brown and sticky lift off on to a rack to cool. Serve plain or sandwiched with cream.

Jalousie

6 oz puff pastry, or trimmings
4 tablespoons home-made jam
** (gooseberry, apricot or plum),**
** or apple marmelade**
1 egg white (beaten)
caster sugar (for dusting)

Method
Set oven at 425°F or Mark 7.

Roll out pastry dough to a large rectangle, ¼ inch thick. Trim and cut out a piece approximately 8 inches by 4 inches. Fold this piece over lengthways and, with a sharp knife, cut across fold at ¼-inch intervals, but not right to outer edges, leaving a border of about 1-1½ inches.

Fold up trimmings and roll out thinly to a rectangle twice the size of folded dough; lift on to dampened baking sheet.

Spoon the jam or marmelade down the centre, spreading it a little. Brush the edges with cold water, then lift the first rectangle of pastry on to it, with the folded edge on the centre. Open out the folded pastry and press the border down on to the lower piece. Cut round edges to neaten, chill for 10 minutes, if necessary, then bake in pre-set oven for 25-30 minutes.

From 5-10 minutes before it's cooked take out of the oven and brush with egg white, beaten to a froth, and dust well with caster sugar. Replace in the oven and remove jalousie when a golden-brown.

Slide on to a rack to cool. Serve hot or cold cut into strips.

Jalousies filled with home-made jam, or brown, sticky palmiers, are delicious and attractive ways of using up puff pastry trimmings

Choux à la crème

choux pastry for 3-4 people
about ½ pint double cream
1 teaspoon caster sugar
icing sugar (for dredging)

For hot chocolate sauce
2 oz chocolate powder
2 tablespoons granulated sugar
1 teaspoon cocoa
½ pint water
3-4 drops of vanilla essence

Method
Set oven at 400°F or Mark 6. Prepare choux pastry. Pipe into small balls or put out with a teaspoon on a dampened baking sheet. Bake for 20-30 minutes on a rising temperature. When quite crisp and firm to the touch, take out and set on a rack to cool.

Make a slit in the side of each ball and fill with the cream, whipped with the teaspoon of caster sugar. Arrange in a pyramid on a serving dish and dust each layer with icing sugar.

To make chocolate sauce: put chocolate powder, sugar, cocoa and water in a pan, stir until sugar is dissolved, then bring to the boil. Simmer sauce for 10-15 minutes or until it is the consistency of cream, rich and syrupy, then add the vanilla. Serve hot sauce separately.

Alternatively, a fruit sauce can be served. Rub fresh soft fruit (eg. raspberries or strawberries) through a nylon strainer. Then sweeten purée with a little icing sugar and dilute with a little water if too thick to pour.

Other suitable fruits are red-currants, blackcurrants, apricots or plums, but these must first be poached and then sieved.

Salambos

choux pastry for 4-6 people

For caramel topping
10 tablespoons caster sugar

For orange cream
4-6 lumps of sugar
1 orange
2-4 drops of rum, or brandy
   (optional)
about ½ pint double cream

Forcing bag; plain éclair pipe

Originally salambos were filled with French pastry cream flavoured with kirsch. The tops were then iced. Here is a variation.

Method
Set oven at 400°F or Mark 6. Prepare choux pastry. Pipe out into balls on dampened baking sheet and bake in oven on a rising temperature for 20-30 minutes until crisp. Prick sides of the balls to release the steam and leave them to cool.

To prepare caramel topping: put caster sugar in a small, heavy pan and cook slowly to a rich brown colour.
Watchpoint Stop the caramel cooking by dipping the bottom of pan in warm water.

When caramel is ready, dip in the top of each choux.

To prepare orange cream: rub sugar lumps over the orange to remove all the zest, then crush them and mix with a little juice to give a rich syrup. Add rum or brandy if wished. Whip the cream lightly and gradually whisk in the orange syrup.
Watchpoint Do not make cream too thick or it will curdle.

Make slits in the sides of the salambos and fill with cream.

Eclairs

choux pastry for 4-6 people
½ pint chocolate, or coffee,
   flavoured pastry cream or
   ½ pint double cream (sweetened
   and flavoured with vanilla
   essence)

For glacé icing
2-3 tablespoons water
2-3 oz plain block chocolate, or
   1-2 tablespoons coffee essence
½-¾ lb icing sugar (sifted)
1-2 tablespoons sugar syrup, or
   water (to mix)

*Forcing bag; ½-inch diameter plain
éclair pipe*

*Piping out choux pastry with an
éclair pipe on to the baking sheet*

Method

Set oven at 400°F or Mark 6.
Prepare choux pastry and pipe
on to dampened baking sheets
in 3-inch lengths. Bake in oven
on a rising temperature for
about 25 minutes until firm and
crisp. Lift off éclairs and prick
to release steam. Leave to cool,
then slit along one side.
   To prepare glacé icing: melt
chocolate in the water in a pan
until it is a smooth cream. Add
sifted icing sugar and stir in
enough sugar syrup or water to
make a thick cream. Have ready
chocolate pastry cream or
whipped cream and pipe into
the éclairs, making sure that the
whole length is filled. Heat the
icing to just over blood heat,
draw aside, then dip in the top
of éclairs. Put on a rack to set.
   For coffee éclairs omit the
chocolate from the pastry
cream and add about 1 tablespoon coffee essence when the
cream has cooled. Omit chocolate from glacé icing and add
instead coffee essence.

69

Strawberry tabatières

choux pastry for 4-6 people
½ lb strawberries
6 tablespoons redcurrant glaze
¼ pint double cream
praline

For pastry cream

1 egg (separated)
1 egg yolk
2 oz caster sugar
2-3 drops of vanilla essence
1 rounded tablespoon plain flour
1 tablespoon cornflour
½ pint milk

Method

Set oven at 400°F or Mark 6.

Make the choux pastry and pipe out on to a dampened baking sheet in the shape of small turnovers and bake on a rising temperature for about 20 minutes until crisp to the touch.

To prepare pastry cream: cream the egg yolks, sugar and vanilla essence together until the mixture looks white; add the flours and a little cold milk and make into a smooth paste. Heat the remaining milk and pour it on to the egg mixture, blend together and return to pan. Stir cream over the heat until boiling, then draw pan aside. Stiffly whip the egg white.

Turn one-third of the pastry cream into a bowl, fold in the egg white gradually, then return mixture to the pan containing the remaining cream and stir gently over heat for 2-3 minutes to set the egg white. Turn cream into a bowl, cover and leave to cool.

Lightly whip cream and fold it into the pastry cream, adding enough praline to flavour it well. Split the cold choux pastry and fill with the praline cream. Arrange the strawberries, dipped in or brushed with warm redcurrant glaze, round the edge of each 'tabatière'.

Tabatière is the French word for a snuff-box, snuff being 'tabac (tobacco) à prise'. This recipe is so called because the choux pastry is folded into a turnover shape, similar to that of a tobacco pouch.

Choux pralinés Montmorency (with cherries)

choux pastry for 4-6 people
1 tablespoon almonds (blanched
   and finely chopped)
½ pint double cream
1 teaspoon caster sugar
4 oz praline
icing sugar (for dredging)

For cherry sauce
1 medium can Morello cherries
   (pitted)
1 dessertspoon arrowroot
1 wineglass red wine
3 tablespoons redcurrant jelly
grated rind of 1 orange

Montmorency is the name
given to a variety of cherry
grown around Paris.

Method
Set oven at 400°F or Mark 6.
   Prepare choux pastry but
reserve about 1 teaspoon of
beaten egg. Pipe out into balls
or put out in rounds with a
dessertspoon on a dampened
baking sheet. Brush top with the
reserved egg and sprinkle with
the chopped almonds. Bake in
the oven on a rising temperature
for about 25 minutes until very
firm to the touch. Prick sides to
release steam and leave to cool.
   Whip cream, sweeten with
caster sugar and fold in the
praline. Make a small hole in
the choux and put the cream
in; dust with icing sugar and
put on a serving dish.
   To make cherry sauce: drain
juice from cherries, blend in the
arrowroot, bring to the boil in
a pan and allow to cool.
   Boil the wine in a pan to
reduce its quantity by half, add
the redcurrant jelly and dissolve
it slowly. Add this to the
thickened cherry juice, and,
when quite cold, stir in the
cherries and grated orange rind.
Serve sauce separately.

Choux pralinés au chocolat

choux pastry for 3-4 people
1 tablespoon almonds (blanched and finely chopped)

For chocolate praline cream
¼ pint milk
1 tablespoon custard powder
3 oz. plain block chocolate
7½ fl oz. double cream (whipped)
4 oz praline

icing sugar (for dredging)

Forcing bag and ½-inch plain éclair pipe

Method

Set oven at 400°F or Mark 6.

Prepare the choux pastry, reserving about 1 teaspoon of beaten egg. Pipe out, using a plain éclair pipe, or put out in dessertspoons on a dampened baking sheet. Brush tops with the reserved beaten egg and sprinkle with chopped almonds. Bake on a rising temperature for 20-25 minutes, until they are golden-brown and quite firm, almost crisp to the touch. Lift choux pastries on to a wire rack to cool and make a small hole in the side of each one.

To prepare chocolate praline cream: blend milk and custard powder, pour into a pan and stir until boiling, beating well. Draw pan aside and leave custard to cool, covered with a dampened greaseproof paper to prevent a skin from forming. Melt chocolate in a pan over gentle heat. When custard is cold, work in the melted chocolate and lastly the whipped cream and praline.

Make a slit in the choux pastries and fill with the chocolate praline mixture. Dust with icing sugar and serve.

*Top: blending melted chocolate with the cold custard before adding cream and praline to make filling
Above: filling choux pastries with the chocolate praline mixture, using a forcing bag and plain pipe*

Chocolate profiteroles

choux pastry for 4-6 people
½ pint chocolate-flavoured pastry
cream

For rich chocolate sauce
6 oz dessert, or bitter, chocolate
½ pint water
4 oz granulated sugar

Forcing bag; plain éclair pipe

Method
Set oven at 400°F or Mark 6.
Prepare choux pastry and pipe
out into small balls or put out
with a teaspoon on a dampened
baking sheet. Bake for 20-30
minutes on a rising temperature
until crisp. Lift profiteroles off
sheets, prick sides to release
steam. Leave to cool.

Prepare chocolate-flavoured
pastry cream and set aside.

Meanwhile make chocolate
sauce: break up the chocolate
and melt in a pan with the water
over a slow heat; when smooth
add the sugar. When sugar is
dissolved, bring to the boil and
simmer with lid off pan for about
10-15 minutes until sauce is
rich, syrupy and of a coating
consistency. Allow to cool.

Make a slit in the profiteroles
and fill with chocolate cream,
using a forcing bag. Pile them
up in a pyramid in a serving dish,
spoon over sauce.

Petits fours

After a rich winter dinner, or to round off a summer buffet, petits fours are just the thing to give a professional touch and make your guests feel they have been offered every possible delicacy. Because of their size—they should be just a mouthful, no more—they are also ideal for afternoon weddings and garden parties. Guests can cope without forks and still have a hand to spare for their champagne glass.

When carefully planned, petits fours are not expensive to make. Like larger pâtisseries, many different types can be made from one batch of foundation, or from the trimmings of something larger. As well as the pastry bases mentioned in other parts of this book, petits fours also make use of fancy biscuit mixtures and meringue cuite. They should be very neatly made and carefully decorated because they must look attractive; it helps, too, if they are served in tiny paper cases.

Unless you are preparing huge quantities of petits fours, it is as well to choose recipes made from only one or two base mixtures; you can then make a reasonable quantity of the mixture and adapt as necessary for each recipe. This saves time, labour and expense. If you are choosing two bases, choose those with contrasting textures, so that some will be crisp, others soft and melting. Arrange them on the tray this way, too, mixing the types to give variety of colour and shape.

Japonais au chocolat

choux pastry for 3-4 people
Chantilly cream (see page 64)
chocolate-flavoured fondant
   icing (made with 8 oz lump
   sugar)
almonds (shredded and
   browned)

Forcing bag; ½-inch plain pipe

Method
Set oven at 400°F or Mark 6.

Pipe the choux pastry into very small rounds on a dampened baking sheet and bake in pre-set oven for about 10 minutes until crisp.

When the cakes are cool, fill with Chantilly cream, using forcing bag, and dip the tops in warm chocolate-flavoured fondant icing. Decorate with the almonds.

Colettes

2 oz plain block chocolate

For ganache cream
2½ oz plain block chocolate
½-¾ oz unsalted butter
4 tablespoons double cream
rum (for flavouring)
gold leaf, or pistachio nuts
   (shredded) – to decorate

*Small sweet cases; forcing bag and
   fine rose pipe*

Method
Cut 2 oz chocolate into small pieces and put on a plate over a pan of hot water. Work with a palette knife until chocolate melts, but do not let it get too hot; allow to cool. Then, using the ball of one finger, line the sweet cases with it. Leave to harden in a cool airy room (not a refrigerator, which would give the chocolate a dull look).

To make ganache cream: break chocolate into pieces and cook in a small pan with the butter and cream until thick, beating well. Flavour with a dash of rum and leave to cool. **Watchpoint** Should the mixture separate, stir in a few drops of cold water.

When chocolate cases are quite firm, remove the paper and pipe in ganache cream.

Decorate with a touch of gold leaf or a shred of pistachio nut.

From top: fours aux amandes, colettes, rochers aux amandes, salambos (glazed and topped with pistachio nuts), coquettes au café, japonais au chocolat

Coquettes au café

meringue cuite (4 egg white quantity)
coffee essence
crystallised, or glacé, cherries

Forcing bag; ½-inch plain pipe

Method
Set oven at 325°F or Mark 3.

Prepare the meringue and flavour with a little strong coffee essence. Put the mixture into a forcing bag and shape into small meringues on an oiled and floured baking sheet, reserving a little in the bag. Bake for about 8 minutes.

When cool, sandwich meringues with a little uncooked meringue mixture and place a small piece of cherry in the middle.

(See photograph showing finished coquettes on page 76.)

1 *Meringue cuite is whisked by hand over hot water to speed up thickening process of the mixture. (Do not whisk over heat if using an electric beater)*

2 *Vanilla-flavoured rochers aux amandes being spooned on to a baking sheet. In the bowl in fore-ground is the coffee-flavoured meringue mixture ready for the coquettes au café*

3 *Piping meringue for coquettes au café on to a baking sheet; in foreground are rochers aux amandes*

Boules de neige

(Snowballs)

1 oz ground almonds
1 oz ground hazelnuts
4 oz icing sugar (plus extra for dredging)
1 egg white (lightly beaten)

Sweet paper cases

Method

Set oven at 325°F or Mark 3.

Pound the nuts together to draw out a little of the oil. Add the sugar gradually and sufficient egg white, a little at a time, to give a paste firm enough to roll in the hand.

Divide the mixture into pieces the size of a large cob nut, roll them in rest of egg white and then in icing sugar. Place in paper cases on baking sheet and bake until well puffed up (about 10 minutes).

Rochers aux amandes

(Almond rocks)

meringue cuite (2 egg white quantity)
1½ oz almonds (finely shredded)
vanilla, or coffee, essence, or chocolate (to flavour)

Method

Set oven at 350°F or Mark 4.

Prepare the meringue, add the almonds and flavouring. Place in heaps on a buttered and floured baking sheet and bake for 8-10 minutes.

Watchpoint When flavouring with chocolate, use a bitter chocolate and melt it without water.

Fours aux amandes

4 oz ground almonds
3 oz caster sugar
2 egg whites
almond, or vanilla, essence
split almonds, or glacé cherries and angelica (to decorate)
1 tablespoon caster sugar (dissolved in 2 tablespoons milk)

Rice paper, or non-stick (silicone) kitchen paper; forcing bag and coarse vegetable rose pipe

Method

Set oven at 350°F or Mark 4.

Mix the almonds and sugar together and pass them through a wire sieve. Whisk egg whites until stiff and fold in the almonds and sugar with the flavouring essence.

Place the non-stick paper, or rice paper (smooth side down), on a dry baking sheet. Fill the forcing bag with the almond mixture. Pipe this on to the paper, making various shapes. Decorate each one with a split almond or glacé cherry and angelica. Bake in pre-set oven for about 15 minutes.

As soon as the cakes are cooked, brush the tops with sugar and milk solution. When cold, break off any surplus rice paper (if used).

Pot pourri

4 oz French flan pastry
trimmings of Madeira, or sponge, cake
1 tablespoon apricot glaze
crystallised fruits, or glacé cherries (finely chopped)
angelica (finely chopped)
candied pineapple (finely chopped) — see page 29
rum (for moistening)
rum-flavoured fondant icing (made with 8 oz lump sugar)
sultanas (to decorate) — optional

8-12 small tartlet tins

Method

Set oven at 375°F or Mark 5. Line tartlet tins with French flan pastry dough, prick the bottom and bake blind for 5 minutes in the pre-set oven.

Meanwhile place in a basin the trimmings of Madeira or sponge cake, a spoonful of apricot glaze, the fruits and a little rum to moisten. Mix well.

When pastry cases are cool, fill with the mixture and then ice with rum-flavoured fondant. Decorate the top of each one with a sultana or leave plain.

Orangines

1½ oz plain flour
2 oz butter
2 oz caster sugar
2 oz almonds (finely chopped)
2 oz candied orange peel (finely chopped)
1 dessertspoon milk
1-2 drops of carmine colouring

Method

Set oven at 350°F or Mark 4 and grease a baking sheet.

Sift the flour. Soften the butter, add sugar to it and beat until white. Add the prepared almonds and candied peel, the flour, milk and carmine, and mix together.

Watchpoint The mixture must be coloured very delicately. The easiest way to do it is to dip a skewer into the carmine bottle and then just to touch the mixture with it.

Put the mixture, ½ teaspoon at a time, on the baking sheet. Flatten the shapes with a wet fork and bake in the pre-set oven until tinged with brown (7-8 minutes). Bake ½ teaspoon of mixture only at first, to test for size. Orangines for petits fours should be no more than 2 inches across.

Leave for 2-3 minutes before removing cooked orangines from the sheet.

Pretzel fondants

4½ oz plain flour
pinch of salt
pinch of ground aniseed, or
  flavouring of choice
2½ oz butter
1 tablespoon caster sugar
1 egg (beaten)
icing sugar (for dredging)

Method

Set oven at 400°F or Mark 6.

Sift the flour with the salt and flavouring on to a pastry board or slab, make a well in the centre and place in this the butter, sugar and egg. Work the dough lightly, as for French flan pastry, and chill for 30 minutes.

Divide dough into pieces the size of a walnut, and roll out on a floured slab so that each piece is the thickness of your little finger in the middle, but thinner at each end. Twist into the traditional pretzel shape (like a loose knot), sticking the ends together with a little beaten egg.

Place the biscuits on a baking sheet and cook in the pre-set oven for 7-8 minutes. Dredge thickly with icing sugar while still hot.

Cooked pretzel fondants dredged with icing sugar

Amaretti secchi

(Dry macaroons)

3½ oz ground almonds
4½ oz caster sugar
1½ oz vanilla sugar
2 egg whites
2 tablespoons kirsch
3-4 almonds (split and shredded)
icing sugar (for dusting)

Non-stick (silicone) kitchen paper

Method

Set oven at 350°F or Mark 4. Pound the almonds and both kinds of sugar with 1 egg white. Whip the second egg white until stiff and fold it into the almond mixture with the kirsch. Divide the mixture into pieces the size of a walnut, roll between the palms of your hands and place on a sheet of non-stick cooking paper on a baking sheet and cook in the pre-set oven for 20-30 minutes. Place a shred of almond on the top of each macaroon and dust with a little icing sugar.

Pains de seigle

4 oz ground almonds
4 oz caster sugar
scant 1 oz plain flour
2 egg whites (lightly beaten)
2 oz praline (pounded and sieved)
icing sugar

Rice paper

This recipe makes about 24 petits fours.

Method

Set the oven at 350°F or Mark 4. Mix the almonds, sugar and flour together and pass them through a wire sieve. Moisten with about three-quarters of the egg whites, adding this gradually and pounding well. Work in the praline.

Divide the mixture into small pieces, each the size of a walnut, roll them first in the remaining egg white and then in a little icing sugar. Bake on rice paper on a baking sheet in the pre-set moderate oven for about 15 minutes. Cool on a wire rack and store in an airtight tin.

Cocktail Savouries

Cocktail time presents some catering difficulties for the cook. Few people want sweet things with cocktails or to eat a full meal while trying to stand up, move around and make conversation among people they don't know. Nevertheless, with drinks around, and possibly strong ones, food is an essential part of the occasion. The knack is in providing not only sufficient quantity, but also sufficient variety.

All too often, guests go home from a cocktail party filled with pastry, rolls and creamy toppings. These things are popular, but need varying with more refreshing items like celery and fruit. And if guests are not going to be eating a main meal for some time, such as at a pre-theatre party, something more substantial such as two or three quiches will be appreciated.

In this section we have tried to suggest some of the more unusual canapés to mix with larger dishes, nuts, crisps and fruit tit-bits.

Presenting cocktail savouries

For cocktail time entertaining, it is worth making an effective arrangement of food for the party to be a real success. This can be achieved by making one large table in the room a focal point with a centrepiece holding a selection of savouries.

Depending on the number of guests invited, a second table can have a variety of hot savouries (on a hotplate or heat tray) and a special dip. Always provide small dishes of salted nuts and olives—plain and stuffed—which can be placed around the room. And you may like to provide something more solid than cocktail snacks by way of sandwiches or bouchées.

For a centrepiece

Choose a good green leaf cabbage. Dip it into boiling water to make the leaves pliable. After draining thoroughly, fold or open back outer leaves and set cabbage on a wooden board. With cocktail sticks pierce small pieces of cheese, cocktail onions, gherkins, small sausages or rolled pieces of bacon etc., and stick them into the hard cabbage heart. Surround the cabbage with small dishes holding an assortment of savouries and in front have a bowl of 'dip' into which plain biscuits, potato crisps or some of the savouries themselves can be dunked.

Quantities for 50 people

Allow 4 canapés per person, and choose 3 or 4 larger dishes for dividing into portions. Also serve some salted nuts, olives and potato crisps; the more substantial snacks should be supplied over and above your selection.

For savoury boat moulds and tartlets

If you search in specialist kitchenware shops you should be able to find very small boat and tartlet moulds. The boat moulds should have a maximum overall measurement of 2 inches, and the tartlet tins be 1½-1¾ inches in diameter. These tins and moulds are best for cocktail use as they make a savoury that is just one mouthful.

To line these moulds see instructions on page 49 Bake blind, lining each with a small piece of crumpled greaseproof paper and a few grains of rice to hold the pastry in position. Bake for about 8 minutes at 375°F or Mark 5.

Savoury almond pastry canapés

Cream cheese and sharp jelly

4 oz quantity savoury almond
   pastry
1 packet (2¾ oz) Demi-Sel, or
   cream cheese
1 oz butter
1 tablespoon hot milk (optional)
salt
piquant jelly (eg. redcurrant)

Forcing bag and small rose pipe

Method
Roll the pastry to ¼ inch thickness and stamp into rounds of 1¼ inches in diameter. Put on a baking sheet lined with greaseproof paper, and bake for 7-8 minutes in a moderate oven, pre-set at 375°F or Mark 5.

Bind the cheese and butter together, adding the hot milk, if necessary, to thin the mixture a little for piping; season to taste with a little salt. Pipe the cheese in a circle around the edges of the canapés. Fill the centres with redcurrant jelly.

Watchpoint To prevent the jelly softening too much, cut it from the jar with a salt spoon, using the spoon as a scoop, and insert it into the centre of each canapé.

Cream cheese and smoked salmon

4 oz quantity savoury almond
   pastry
about 3 oz cream, or curd,
   cheese
salt and pepper
about 1 tablespoon hot milk
2 oz smoked salmon
black pepper (ground from mill)
squeeze of lemon juice

Forcing bag and vegetable rose pipe

Method
Roll out the almond pastry dough to ¼ inch thick and cut into oblongs 2 inches by 1 inch, then bake in oven, pre-set at 375°F or Mark 5, for 5-6 minutes.

Work the cheese with seasoning and hot milk to make a good consistency for piping. Put this into the forcing bag. Next chop the smoked salmon.

Watchpoint It is best to chop the salmon rather carefully with a serrated knife, cutting it first into thin strips and then crossways into very small dice. As smoked salmon is very oily, it tends to stick together if chopped in the usual way.

Season the salmon with black pepper and a little lemon juice. Pipe the cream cheese over the top of each canapé and sprinkle with the prepared smoked salmon.

Tartlets niçoise

There are various fillings that can be used for these tartlets; here we give four. Allow 4 oz savoury almond pastry for each batch of tartlets, and bake blind in the appropriate moulds or tins for 8 minutes at 375°F or Mark 5. The first two fillings are for pastry boat moulds, and the second two are for round tartlets.

Filling 1

1 clove of garlic (cut)
2 oz unsalted butter
½ teaspoon tomato purée
salt and pepper
sugar (to taste)
squeeze of lemon juice

For garnish
1 tablespoon finely chopped
   parsley
1 tablespoon finely chopped
   browned almonds

Method

Rub a small bowl with the cut garlic, then soften the butter in this. Add the tomato purée and season with salt, pepper, sugar and lemon juice to taste. Fill this mixture into the baked pastry cases, doming it well and shaping it to an inverted V with a knife blade. Place the chopped parsley along one side and chopped almonds along the other.

Filling 2

2 oz curd, or cottage, cheese
½ oz butter
salt and pepper
4 black olives (finely chopped)

For garnish
1 hard-boiled egg

Method

Work the cheese with the butter until smooth, season and add the chopped olives. Fill this mixture into the baked pastry cases, shaping it in the same way as for filling 1.

Arrange sieved egg yolk down one side and finely chopped egg white down the other.

Filling 3

half 4 oz can of sardines
little vinaigrette dressing
1 teaspoon chopped capers

For garnish
1 tomato (skinned and sliced)

Method

Drain the sardines carefully. Scrape away the skin, then remove the bone and tail. Mash the sardines, mixing with a very little vinaigrette and adding the capers. Place this mixture in the baked pastry cases. Smooth the top of the mixture absolutely level. Cover each tartlet with a slice of tomato.

Filling 4

half 3½-4 oz can of tunny fish
1 tablespoon thick mayonnaise
salt and pepper

For garnish
1 hard-boiled egg (sliced)
cucumber slices (lightly salted)

Method
Pound the tunny fish and mayonnaise together until smooth, seasoning well. Fill the mixture into the baked pastry cases and smooth the top. Place a slice of hard-boiled egg on each one, drain the cucumber slices and place them on top of the slices of egg.

Petites bouchées écossaises

4 oz quantity of puff pastry
1 egg (beaten)

For filling
1 packet (2¾ oz) Demi-Sel cheese
1 tablespoon double cream
3 oz smoked salmon (shredded)
black pepper (ground from mill)
squeeze of lemon juice

Fluted cutters (1½-inch and 1-inch diameter)

This quantity will make 8-9 small bouchées.

Method
Set oven at 425°F or Mark 7.
Roll out the puff pastry dough to no more than ¼ inch thick for these little bouchées.
Cut dough into rounds or ovals with the larger fluted cutter. Set on a dampened baking sheet and brush with beaten egg. Mark a smaller circle in the centre of each bouchée for the lid. Chill for 10 minutes before baking in pre-set oven for 10-15 minutes.
To prepare the filling: beat the cheese until smooth, soften with the cream and add the shredded salmon; season with black pepper and lemon juice to taste.
When the bouchées are baked remove the tops and scoop away any soft pastry from the inside; allow to cool, then fill with the cheese and salmon mixture. Replace bouchée tops.

Small devilled croissants

about 6 oz quantity of puff pastry

For filling
2 oz ham (finely chopped)
1 tablespoon firm type of pickle
1 teaspoon mayonnaise
few drops of Tabasco sauce
little beaten egg

These croissants are ideal for using up puff pastry trimmings, and this quantity will make about 12 croissants.

Method

Set the oven at 425°F or Mark 7. Mix ham, pickle and mayonnaise together for the filling and season well with Tabasco.

Roll out the puff pastry dough into a long narrow strip, trim the edges and cut into 3-inch squares. Cut each square in half diagonally and put ½ teaspoon of the savoury filling on each triangle. Roll up and make into a crescent, place on a dampened baking sheet. Brush with beaten egg and bake in the pre-set oven for 8-10 minutes, or until golden-brown and crisp.

Kartoffelstangen

½ lb potatoes (peeled)
8 oz butter
8 oz plain flour
salt and pepper
egg wash
dill, or caraway seeds

Method

Boil the potatoes until tender, drain and dry very thoroughly, then crush with a potato masher or fork until quite smooth. Have the butter at room temperature in a warm basin, add the potatoes. Sift in the flour with plenty of seasoning; work together, first with a palette knife and then with the hand, to a soft dough.

Chill for at least 1 hour. Set the oven at 400°F or Mark 6. Roll out chilled dough to a rectangle, trim the sides. Brush dough with an egg wash and sprinkle the top with dill or caraway seeds. Cut into sticks ¼ inch wide and 3-4 inches long; bake in the pre-set oven for about 10-15 minutes, until golden-brown and crisp.

Savoury petits choux

For choux pastry
¼ pint water
2 oz butter
2½ oz plain flour
salt and pepper
pinch of cayenne pepper
2 eggs

To finish
little beaten egg
little Parmesan cheese (grated)

Forcing bag and vegetable pipe

These petits choux should be filled — at the last possible moment—with one of the three fillings which follow this recipe. This quantity will make about 18 petits choux.

Method
Set the oven at 400°F or Mark 6. Prepare choux pastry, sifting seasoning in with the flour. Using the vegetable pipe, pipe out the mixture into very small balls on to a dampened baking sheet. Brush the top of each ball with a little beaten egg and dust with Parmesan cheese.

Bake in the pre-set oven for about 12 minutes, or until very crisp to the touch. Remove from oven, prick sides to release steam and leave to cool.

Just before serving make a small hole in the side of each choux and pipe in chosen filling.

Filling 1

1 oz cream cheese
1 tablespoon chopped celery
1 tablespoon chopped green
    pepper (blanched and
    drained)
1 teaspoon chopped chives
1 teaspoon tomato ketchup
salt and pepper
little cream (optional)

Method
Work all the ingredients together and season well, adding a little cream if necessary to make a good consistency.

Filling 2

1 oz cream cheese
salt and pepper
squeeze of lemon juice
1 tablespoon cream
2 oz potted shrimps

Method
Work the cream cheese with the seasoning, lemon juice and cream, add potted shrimps.

Filling 3

2-3 oz cooked chicken
    trimmings (finely diced)
1 tablespoon thick mayonnaise
1 oz cooked tongue (chopped) —
    optional

Method
Bind the chicken with the mayonnaise. Add the tongue, if wished, to give extra flavour.

Cheese beignets

choux pastry for 3-4 people
2 tablespoons finely grated cheese

grated Parmesan cheese
  (to finish)
cayenne pepper

Deep fat bath

Method

Make choux pastry and mix in
the 2 tablespoons grated cheese
after adding the second egg.
The dough must be firm enough
to keep its shape.

Divide it into heaped tea-
spoonfuls on a tin or dish. Heat
the fat bath to 370°F. Dip a
palette knife in the fat and use
this to lift each teaspoon of
pastry from the tin to the fat.
Leave plenty of room for beignets to swell, and to turn over
while cooking.

Once the beignets begin to
puff out, increase heat gradually
and continue cooking for about
8 minutes, until golden-brown
and firm to the touch.

Lift out beignets with a draining spoon and drain them on
absorbent paper. Dust with
grated Parmesan cheese and
cayenne before serving.

Marjolaine tartlets

4 oz quantity of rich shortcrust
   pastry
choux pastry for 3-4 people
2 oz Cheddar cheese (grated)
salt and pepper

For cheese sauce

½ oz butter
1 tablespoon plain flour
½ pint milk (infused with 1 bayleaf,
   1 slice of onion, 1 blade of mace,
   6 peppercorns)
1½ oz cheese (grated)
salt and pepper

*6-8 tartlet tins; forcing bag and small
   round pipe*

Method
Line the tins with rich shortcrust pastry dough. Prick bottoms and bake blind for 10-15
minutes in oven at 375°F or
Mark 5.

Prepare choux pastry, stirring
in cheese and seasoning after
adding second egg. Pipe choux
into shortcrust pastry tartlets,
leaving a hollow in the middle
of each one. Increase oven heat
to 400°F or Mark 6.

To prepare cheese sauce:
melt butter in a pan, stir in flour
and cook to a pale-straw
colour. Strain milk, stir it on to
the flour mixture and simmer for
2 minutes. Season and add
cheese.

Pour sauce into hollow in
middle of tartlets and bake in
pre-set oven for 15-20 minutes
to cook choux pastry gently,
while browning the cheese in
the middle of the tartlets. Serve
immediately.

Roulades

4 oz quantity savoury shortcrust
   pastry
French mustard
paprika pepper
Gentleman's Relish (Patum
   Pepperium)
1-2 tablespoons grated
   Parmesan cheese

Method
Roll out the shortcrust pastry
dough very thinly, to about ⅛
inch thick, and spread thinly
with French mustard, dust with
paprika and then spread with
a little Gentleman's Relish and
sprinkle the cheese over the top.

Roll pastry up as for a swiss
roll, wrap in waxed or greaseproof paper and chill for 30
minutes. Cut the roll into ¼ inch
thick slices (or thinner if possible) and place flat on a baking
sheet lined with greaseproof
paper. Bake for about 8 minutes
in a moderate oven, pre-set
at 375°F or Mark 5.

Lobster tartlets

(Bateaux de homard)

4 oz quantity savoury shortcrust
    pastry
3-4 oz cooked lobster (fresh or
    canned)
French dressing
chopped celery (about half
    quantity of lobster)
1 teaspoon chopped parsley
1-2 tablespoons thick
    mayonnaise
2 tablespoons chopped
    watercress

12-16 boat moulds

Method

Line boat moulds with pastry
dough, prick bottoms, and bake
blind.

Cut the lobster meat into
small pieces and leave to soak
in a little French dressing while
baking the boat moulds.

Drain the lobster and mix it
with the celery and parsley,
and add just enough mayonnaise to bind the mixture together. Fill it into the cooled
boat moulds and cover the top
with the chopped watercress.

Feuilletées

8 oz puff pastry
10-12 oz Roquefort cheese
1 egg (beaten)

Method

Set oven at 425°F or Mark 7.
Roll out the pastry dough to a
piece about 12-14 inches long
and 8 inches wide.

Cut the Roquefort into eight
'fingers' about 3 inches long,
brush half of the pastry with
water and lay the cheese on
this at intervals. Cover with the
other half of the pastry, pressing
it down well between each
piece of cheese. Cut out the
'fingers' and brush lightly with
beaten egg.

Bake in pre-set oven for
15-20 minutes. Serve hot.

Sweet flans, pies and tarts

English and American pies and tarts are on the whole plainer than those from continental Europe, but no less delicious in their way. Shortcrust and American pie pastry are used, and the richer flaky and puff pastries.

An English pie is made in a deep dish, with a lid of pastry on top. Following the custom of the old days, when meat and fruit pies were all baked together in a batch, in one large oven, sweet pies are left plain to distinguish them from the highly ornamented meat ones. Alternatively, an English pie may be a 'plate pie' in a shallow plate, with pastry underneath and on top. Firm fruit such as apples, gooseberries and blackcurrants are best in these, and plate pies should be placed on a hot baking sheet in the oven in order to cook the pastry underneath.

The word tart is often used instead of pie, but correctly a tart is open, with pastry on the bottom and fruit or another filling on top. Like a pie, it is served in the dish in which it is cooked.

A flan is a particularly attractive variation on the usual tart, as the ring which holds it in place during cooking is removed for serving. The pastry, usually shortcrust or French flan pastry, is rolled out and lined on to a flan ring on a baking sheet. If you don't have a flan ring, you can, of course, use a sandwich tin with a loose bottom, but to avoid breaking the pastry or burning yourself, leave it to cool before removing it from the tin.

If you are using apples, gooseberries or stone fruit in a flan, cook them in the raw pastry case. If you are using soft fruits or fruit which has already been poached, bake the flan blind and arrange the fruit in the cooked flan. Once filled, glaze with either thickened fruit juice, or a jam or jelly glaze. For serving, don't forget to use a flat plate or a board, not a shallow dish, or your flan will collapse into the hollow of the dish.

Apple pie

8 oz shortcrust pastry
caster sugar (for dusting)

For filling
1½ lb cooking or mildly acid
   dessert apples
1 strip of lemon rind
2-3 rounded tablespoons sugar
   (brown or white)
little grated lemon rind, or 1-2
   cloves

8-inch diameter pie dish

This is one of the oldest of English dishes and delicious when properly made. Use a fair-sized dish that holds plenty of fruit. Apples may be cookers, preferably a variety that will retain shape when cooked, or a mildly acid dessert apple such as Cox's orange pippin. A Blenheim orange apple, though not easy to find these days, makes an excellent pie, and combines both the qualities of dessert and cooking apples.

Method
To get the most flavour, peel, quarter and core the apples, keeping them in a covered bowl (not in water) while making juice from the cores and peel. Put these last in a pan with a strip of lemon rind, barely cover with water and simmer for 15-20 minutes. Then strain. (Water can, of course, be used in place of the juice made from the peel.)

While the juice is simmering, prepare shortcrust pastry. Put in the refrigerator to chill, or set aside in a cool place for about 30 minutes.

Cut apple quarters into 2-3 pieces, pack into pie dish.

Watchpoint Do not slice the apples too thinly or the juice will run too quickly and may render the slices tough and tasteless.

Layer these slices with 2-3 tablespoons of sugar, according to the acidity of the fruit. Add, too, a little grated lemon rind or 1-2 cloves. Dome the fruit slightly above the edge of the dish (this is sufficient to prevent the pastry top from falling in, so there is no need to use a pie funnel). Pour in enough of the strained apple juice (or water) to half fill dish.

Take up the pastry dough and roll out to about ¼ inch thick, cut a strip or two from the sides and lay these on dampened edge of the pie dish. Press down and brush them with water. Take up the rest of the dough on the rolling pin and lay it over the pie. Press down the edge, then lift the dish up on one hand and cut the excess pastry away, holding the knife slantwise towards the bottom of the dish to get a slightly overhanging edge. Pinch or scallop round the edge with your fingers, brush the pastry lightly with water, dust with caster sugar (a dry glaze), or leave plain and dust with caster sugar after baking.

Set the pie on a baking sheet for ease of putting in and taking out of the oven, and to catch any juice that may spill over. Bake for about 25 minutes on the centre shelf of the oven, pre-set at 375-400°F or Mark 5-6, when the pastry should be brown. Then lower the oven temperature to 350°F or Mark 4 for a further 10-15 minutes to complete cooking.

Bakewell tart

6 oz rich shortcrust pastry

For filling
1 tablespoon strawberry jam
1 tablespoon lemon curd
1 oz butter
2 oz caster sugar
grated rind and juice of ½ lemon
1 egg
2 oz ground almonds
2 rounded tablespoons cake
   crumbs

7-inch diameter sandwich tin

Method
Make the rich shortcrust pastry
dough and set aside to chill.
When chilled, roll it out and line
the sandwich tin, trim edge and
scallop with the thumb. Spread
the pastry first with jam and then
with lemon curd.

Cream the butter in a bowl
until soft, add the sugar and
lemon rind and continue beating until light. Beat egg, add a
little at a time, and then stir in
the almonds, cake crumbs and
lemon juice. Spread the almond
mixture over the lemon curd and
bake for 35-45 minutes until
set and golden-brown in an
oven pre-set at 375°F or Mark 5.

Treacle tart

For very rich shortcrust
6 oz plain flour
pinch of salt
1 teaspoon baking powder
3 oz butter
2 oz lard, or shortening

For filling
3 rounded tablespoons fresh white
   breadcrumbs
1 teacup golden syrup
grated rind and juice of ½ lemon

Large ovenproof plate

Rich shortcrust can be used for
treacle tart but this recipe has
an even richer pastry (which
should only be used for a plate
pie). Baking powder is added to
lighten the pastry somewhat,
as there is a heavy quantity of fat.

Method
Sift the flour, salt and baking
powder together. Rub in the
fats lightly and quickly, then
press the dough firmly together.
Knead, roll out, line on to ovenproof plate. Trim round the edge
and set aside to chill. Set oven
at 375°F or Mark 5.

Mix the crumbs, syrup, lemon
rind and juice together. Turn on
to the plate, roll out the trimmings and cut into strips. Twist
these and lay over the syrup
mixture, lattice-fashion. Press a
strip of dough round the edge
of the plate to neaten. Bake for
35-45 minutes in pre-set oven.
Lower heat slightly once pastry
has begun to colour, and continue cooking until well
browned. Serve on the plate in
which it is cooked.

Bavarian apple tart

For rich shortcrust
6 oz plain flour
pinch of salt
4 oz butter
1½ rounded tablespoons caster
　sugar
1 egg yolk
3-4 tablespoons milk
icing sugar (for dusting)

For apple mixture
1-1½ lb cooking apples
1 rounded tablespoon currants
1 rounded tablespoon sultanas
2 tablespoons fresh white
　breadcrumbs
1-2 tablespoons sugar
　(brown, or white)
1 teaspoon ground cinnamon

Method
Prepare the pastry, adding the milk in place of water. Set aside to chill. Set oven at 375°F or Mark 5.

Peel, core and slice the apples. Put into a bowl with the cleaned, dried fruit, crumbs, sugar and cinnamon, and mix well.

Knead pastry lightly to work out any cracks, and roll out thinly to a rectangle about 9 inches by 6 inches. Slide on to a baking sheet (preferably one without edges which makes it easier to remove the tart after cooking). Trim the pastry edges, then place the apple mixture down the middle, leaving about 1½-2 inches of pastry on each side. Lift these sides up and over with a palette knife, so that they rest on the mixture, but leave a gap in the middle to show the filling. Press the pastry down lightly with the knife so that the sides remain in place while baking.

Bake for 35-40 minutes in pre-set oven. Slide on to a rack to cool, then dust thickly with icing sugar before cutting into slices for serving.

Serve with cream or custard separately, or a mixture of thick custard and yoghourt whisked together. Do this when the custard is cold and well sweetened, adding the yoghourt to taste.

Pastry finishes

Here are some guide-points to give your pastry a professional finish.

1 When only one layer of pastry is used, **forking** edge is adequate. Press back of fork prongs into edges.

2a When two layers are used, seal edges by placing side of left forefinger on top of pie and, with back of broad-bladed knife, make indentations in double edges. This prevents layers splitting when baked.

2b To decorate, flute by pressing left thumb on top of outer edge. Draw back of knife towards centre for ½ inch, repeating all way round. Leave ¾ inch between cuts for savoury pies, ¼ inch for sweet ones.

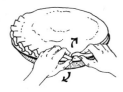

3 Crimp by pinching pastry edge between thumb and forefinger of each hand, twisting slightly in opposite directions.

Cherry pie

8 oz American pie pastry
1 egg white (for glazing)
cream (optional)

For filling
2½ cups cherries (fresh or canned,
    stewed and stoned)
8 fl oz cherry juice
2 rounded tablespoons caster
    sugar
1 tablespoon melted butter
1 tablespoon fine tapioca, or sago
2 drops of almond essence

7-8 inch diameter pie plate about
   2½ inches deep

Method

Make pastry dough and set aside to chill. Either fresh or canned Morello or red cherries (ie. not too sweet) are best for this pie. If fresh cherries are used, stone and cook in a little sugar syrup, and drain well.

Mix all the ingredients for the filling together and allow to stand for 15 minutes. Set the oven at 400°F or Mark 6. Line the dough on to the pie plate, pour in the fruit mixture and cover with the remaining pastry. Bake for 30-40 minutes in pre-set oven.

Take pie out of the oven, brush with lightly whisked egg white and dust with caster sugar. Put back in the oven and bake for a further 5-7 minutes. Serve hot or cold, with cream.

Deep South apple pie

8 oz American pie pastry
cream (optional)
caster sugar (for dusting)

For filling
1½-2 lb cooking apples
4-5 oz sugar (brown or white)
½ teaspoon cinnamon
1 tablespoon orange marmalade
½ oz butter

7-8 inch diameter pie plate about 2 inches deep

Method
Make pastry dough and set aside to chill. Peel, core and slice apples. Cook with the sugar and cinnamon to a thick pulp. Add marmalade and butter, beat well and continue to cook for 5 minutes longer, stirring frequently. Turn out to cool. Set oven at 400°F or Mark 6.

Divide the pastry in two. Roll out and line one piece on to the pie plate. Fill with the apple mixture, then cover with the other piece, brush the pastry lightly with water and dust with caster sugar. Bake for 30-40 minutes in the pre-set oven.

Serve hot or cold, with plenty of thick cream.

To cook pumpkin
You will need about 1 lb raw pumpkin to make ½ lb cooked. Peel the pumpkin, cut it up, removing seeds, and stew gently in a little water until tender (about 15 minutes). Strain and mash; use as required.

American pumpkin pie

For shortcrust pastry
8 oz self-raising flour
pinch of salt
5 oz shortening (Spry or Trex)
about 5 tablespoons cold water

For filling
½ lb mashed cooked pumpkin
4 oz soft brown sugar
pinch of salt
1 teaspoon ground cinnamon
½ teaspoon ground ginger
¼ teaspoon ground nutmeg
2 eggs
½ pint creamy milk

Deep 8-inch diameter pie plate

This is a traditional American recipe.

Method
Make up the pastry dough and line the pie plate. The edge of the pie should be high and fluted and to do this, line the sides and top edge of the plate with two layers of pastry. Press these together firmly and chill well while preparing the filling, then flute or crimp the edge (see page 97). Set oven at 375°F or Mark 5.

Mix the sugar, salt and spices together. Beat the eggs and stir in the milk and mashed pumpkin. Add the sugar and spices to the pumpkin mixture and pour into the uncooked pastry case.

Bake in the pre-set oven for 45-50 minutes, or until a knife inserted in the filling comes out clean. Leave pie to cool a little before serving.

Pumpkin pie Cordon Bleu

8 oz quantity of shortcrust pastry
(as for American pumpkin pie,
page 99)

For filling

½ lb mashed cooked pumpkin
(see page 99)
4 oz soft brown sugar
1 tablespoon thick honey
grated rind and juice of 1 lemon
grated rind and juice of 1 orange
2 eggs (well beaten)

To finish

¼ pint double cream
1 teaspoon caster sugar
¼ teaspoon grated nutmeg
2 oz walnuts (roughly chopped),
or almonds (shredded and
toasted)

Deep 8-inch diameter pie plate

A Cordon Bleu variation on a traditional American recipe

Method

Line the pie plate with pastry dough as in American pumpkin pie on page 99. Set oven at 375°F or Mark 5.

To prepare filling: mix the sugar, honey and fruit juices together, add the beaten eggs and the grated fruit rinds, then stir in the mashed pumpkin. Pour the mixture into the prepared pastry case and bake in pre-set oven for 45-55 minutes, or until a knife inserted in filling comes out clean. Allow to cool.

Whip the cream, sweeten it with the sugar and add the nutmeg. Just before serving, cover the pie with the cream and sprinkle with chopped nuts.

Lemon chiffon pie

American crumb shell (see right),
   or 6-8 oz quantity rich shortcrust
   pastry

For filling
2 eggs (separated)
4 oz caster sugar
pinch of salt
juice of 1 small lemon and
   grated rind of ½ lemon
1 teaspoon powdered gelatine
   (soaked in 1 tablespoon cold
   water)
pinch of cream of tartar
1 small carton (2½ fl oz) double
   cream

*8-inch diameter pie plate, or 8-inch
diameter flan ring (buttered)*

Method
Line the pie plate or flan ring
with American crumb shell or
shortcrust pastry dough and
bake blind.

   Beat egg yolks with 2 oz sugar,
salt, lemon juice and rind;
pour all into a double saucepan,
cook and stir until thick. Remove the pan from the heat,
add the soaked gelatine, stir
in well and leave to cool.

   Whisk the egg whites with the
cream of tartar until foaming,
then add the remaining sugar
a dessertspoon at a time, and
continue whisking until stiff and
glossy. Whisk the cream until
thick.

   When the lemon mixture begins to set, beat with a rotary
whisk until smooth and then
fold it into the meringue with
the cream.

   Pile the mixture into the
cooled pie shell or flan and chill
until set. Take out of the refrigerator 20 minutes before serving.

American crumb shell

5 oz biscuit crumbs
4 oz caster sugar
4 oz butter (melted)

*8-inch diameter pie plate 2-2½ inches
deep, or 8-inch diameter flan ring*

This pie crust is very popular
and is used with fresh fruit and
cream or chiffon pies. Make
with an unsweetened biscuit—
a Cornish wafer is very suitable.

Method
Crush the biscuits with a rolling
pin and rub them through a
wire sieve or strainer into a
mixing bowl. Add the sugar and
melted butter. Press the mixture
thickly over bottom and sides of
buttered pie plate or flan ring.

   Chill pie crust before filling or,
alternatively, bake blind for 10
minutes in oven pre-set at 375°F
or Mark 5 and then chill.

*American crumb shell is pressed
down to coat flan ring thickly*

Fruit crust pies with apple or peach filling

For American pastry

11 oz plain flour
7 oz lard, or shortening
4 tablespoons water
¼ teaspoon salt

For apple filling

2 lb Pippin apples (peeled and
  cored)
½ teaspoon freshly ground
  cinnamon
grated rind and juice of 1 lemon
little butter

For peach filling

1 large can sliced peaches
4 fresh peaches
little butter

Two 7-8 inch diameter pie plates

This quantity of pastry will make two pies.

Method

To make the American pastry, put the lard (or shortening) and water into a mixing bowl and work together with a wooden spoon until creamy. Sift the flour with the salt into the bowl and cut and stir with a round-bladed knife until all the ingredients are well blended. Gather the dough together with the fingertips, press it firmly into a ball, wrap it in waxed paper and chill before using.

Divide the pastry dough in four, and roll out two pieces into rounds about ⅛ inch thick and 1 inch larger than the pie plates to allow for depth. Keep the dough round as it is being rolled and be careful not to add extra flour as this will make it tough. Fold the rounds in half, or lift them one at a time on the rolling pin, and quickly line them into the pie plates. Avoid stretching the pastry, and trim the edges with a knife or scissors.

Set the oven at 425°F or Mark 7. Slice the apples, and fill one of the pies, doming the fruit, and add the cinnamon and lemon juice.

For the other pie, drain the canned peaches well; scald, peel and slice the fresh peaches and mix them with the canned ones. Fill the pie.

Dot both fruits with butter, and moisten the edges of the pastry with water.

Roll out the remaining pieces of pastry a little thinner than the bottom crusts and 1 inch larger than the plates. Fold in half. Make several slits across the centre fold and lift carefully on to the pies. Unfold the pastry and fold the overhanging pastry under the lower layer. Seal the edges and flute with your forefinger and thumb (see page 97).

Bake in the pre-set oven for 15 minutes, then reduce the heat to 400°F or Mark 6, and bake for a further 20-30 minutes. Serve warm.

Flans

There are two types of flan ring, the 1 inch deep British one and the true French kind which is barely ¾ inch deep. This latter ring is the correct one for all fruit flans and can be found in specialist shops. The deeper ring is good for savoury flans, where a generous amount of filling is used. A flan can be made in a loose-bottomed sandwich tin, but to avoid breaking pastry, or burning yourself, leave it to cool before removing from the tin.

Apples, gooseberries and stone fruit may be cooked in the raw pastry flan. Other fruits, such as raspberries or poached fruit, are arranged in the pre-cooked flan (baked blind).

Lining a flan ring

1 Have ready the dough, well chilled. Set the flan ring on a baking sheet, preferably without edges, for easy removal of the flan. Roll out the dough to a thickness of ¼-½ inch, according to the recipe, and to a diameter about 1½ inches bigger than the flan ring. Lift dough on the rolling pin and lay it over the flan ring, quickly easing it down into the ring.

2 Take a small ball of the dough, dip in flour and press into the ring, especially round the bottom edge.

3 Now bend back the top edge and roll off excess dough with the rolling pin (see photograph).

4 Pinch round the edge with the side of the forefinger and thumb, then push the dough (with the fingers) up the side

Lifting the dough on rolling pin before laying it over the flan ring

Rolling off the excess pastry dough

Pinching the edge of dough with forefinger and thumb after raising it ▶ 103

Flans continued

from the bottom of the ring to increase the height of the edge. Prick the base of the flan several times with a fork. Then fill with raw fruit.

Baking blind

1 A flan case should be pre-cooked before filling with soft or cooked fruit. Once the flan ring is lined with pastry dough, chill for about 30 minutes to ensure the dough is well set.

2 Line the dough with crumpled greaseproof paper, pressing it well in at the bottom edge and sides.

3 Three-parts fill the flan with uncooked rice or beans (to hold the shape) and put into the oven to bake. An 8-inch diameter flan ring holding a 6-8 oz quantity of pastry should cook for about 26 minutes in an oven at 400°F or Mark 6.

4 After about 20 minutes of the cooking time take flan out of the oven and carefully remove the paper and rice, or beans. (Beans may be used many times over for baking blind.) Replace the flan in the oven to complete cooking. The ring itself can either be taken off with the paper and rice,. or removed after cooking. Once cooked, slide the flan on to a wire rack and then leave to cool.

Before baking blind, line the flan with greaseproof paper, then three-parts fill with beans or rice

Gâteau basque

For rich shortcrust pastry
6 oz plain flour
pinch of salt
1 oz shortening
3 oz butter
3 rounded dessertspoons ground
  almonds
6 dessertspoons caster sugar
1 egg yolk
2-3 drops of vanilla essence
2-3 tablespoons cold water

For filling
4-5 heaped tablespoons jam
  (preferably plum, gooseberry,
  damson, etc.)
1 egg white (lightly beaten)
caster sugar (for dusting)

6-7 inch diameter flan ring

Method

Prepare rich shortcrust pastry dough, adding the almonds with the sugar and mixing the vanilla with the egg yolk and water. Chill slightly. Set oven at 400°F or Mark 6.

Roll out two-thirds of the dough to ¼-½ inch thickness and line the flan ring. Fill with the jam, roll out the rest of the dough to a round and lay over the top. Press down the edges, mark the surface, cart-wheel-fashion, with the point of a knife. Bake for 30-35 minutes in pre-set oven. Lower oven temperature to 375°F or Mark 5 after the first 15 minutes.

Just before the gâteau is ready, brush the top with a little lightly beaten egg white, dust immediately with caster sugar and return to the oven for about 2 minutes to frost the top. Serve hot or cold.

Watchpoint The sugar must be dusted on to the egg white quickly, before the heat of the pastry has a chance to set the egg white, so that the sugar and egg white combine to make a meringue-like topping of frost.

Lemon meringue pie

For rich shortcrust pastry
6 oz plain flour
pinch of salt
3½ oz butter
1 egg yolk
1-2 tablespoons cold water

For filling
1 rounded tablespoon cornflour
½ pint milk
1 rounded tablespoon caster sugar
2 egg yolks
grated rind and juice of 1 lemon

For meringue
2 egg whites
4 oz caster sugar

7-inch diameter flan ring

Method

Make the rich shortcrust pastry dough and set aside to chill. Then roll out, line the flan ring and bake blind.

Mix the cornflour with a little of the milk in a bowl and heat the rest of the milk in saucepan. Pour on to the mixed cornflour, return to the pan and boil for 3-4 minutes, stirring continuously to make it smooth.

Add the sugar, allow to cool a little, beat in the egg yolks, the grated lemon rind and juice. Pour this mixture into the pastry case; bake for about 10 minutes at 325°F or Mark 3 to set.

To make meringue: whisk the egg whites with a fork or wire whisk until stiff and dry. Whisk in 2 teaspoons of the sugar and then carefully fold in the remainder with a metal spoon.

Watchpoint Whisking in this small quantity of sugar helps set the whites and folding in the bulk is important to avoid knocking out the air beaten into the whites. If you overstir, the sugar starts to liquefy and the egg whites collapse, resulting in a rather thin layer of meringue which is also tough on the top.

Pile the meringue on the top of pie to cover the filling completely, dredge with caster sugar. To set meringue, place in a cool oven for 10-15 minutes at 275°F or Mark 1. The consistency of a meringue topping should be that of a marshmallow, firm to cut, yet soft and with a crisp coating.

Chocolate meringue pie

6-8 oz quantity rich shortcrust
  pastry

For filling
2 oz cocoa
4 oz granulated sugar
pinch of salt
2 tablespoons cornflour
1 dessertspoon plain flour
1 pint milk
2 egg yolks (beaten)
1 oz butter
3-4 drops of vanilla essence

For meringue
2 egg whites
pinch of cream of tartar
4 oz caster sugar

8-inch diameter flan ring

Method
Line the flan ring with the pastry
dough and bake blind. Set oven
at 340°F or Mark 4.

Put the cocoa, sugar, salt,
cornflour and flour in a saucepan and mix them to a smooth
paste with the milk. Stir over
gentle heat until boiling and
cook for 1 minute. Pour half the
mixture on to the beaten egg
yolks, return this to remainder
in the pan and cook for 1 minute.
Beat in the butter and vanilla
essence and pour mixture into
prepared pastry flan.

Now prepare the meringue:
whisk the egg whites with the
cream of tartar until foaming,
add the sugar gradually and
continue whisking until stiff and
glossy. Pile this on to the
chocolate filling, being careful
to seal the meringue on to the
pastry and so prevent shrinking.
Bake in pre-set oven for 8-10
minutes or until lightly browned.

Butterscotch cream pie

6-8 oz rich shortcrust pastry

For filling
2 oz butter
4 oz dark brown sugar
¼ pint boiling water
2 tablespoons cornflour
1 tablespoon plain flour
large pinch of salt
½ pint milk
2 egg yolks (beaten)
2 drops of vanilla essence

To decorate
¼ pint double cream (whipped)
2 tablespoons almonds (browned
  and finely chopped)

8-inch diameter flan ring

Method
Line the flan ring with the
pastry dough, bake blind and
chill cooked flan case.

Melt the butter in a heavy
frying pan or saucepan and
when golden-brown add the
brown sugar; stir until foaming
and boil for 2-3 minutes. Remove from the heat and stir in
the boiling water.

Place the cornflour, flour and
salt in a saucepan and mix to a
smooth paste with the milk,
then add the brown sugar
mixture. Stir over gentle heat
until boiling and then cook for
1 minute.

Pour half the mixture on to
the beaten egg yolks, return
this to remainder in the pan and
continue cooking for 1 minute;
add vanilla essence. Pour the
mixture into the baked pastry
flan and chill again.

Cover the top with the whipped cream and decorate with
the almonds.

Cornish treacle tart

6 oz flaky pastry (well chilled)

For filling
8 tablespoons fresh white
    breadcrumbs
1 teacup golden syrup
grated rind and juice of ½ lemon
caster sugar (for dusting)

*6-7 inch diameter sandwich tin, or
    pie plate*

Method
Set oven at 425°F or Mark 7.
    Mix the breadcrumbs, syrup,
and lemon rind and juice together. Roll out the pastry dough
to an oblong 12 inches by 7
inches and cut in two. Roll one
piece a little thinner, line the
tin or pie plate with it and damp
the edges.
    Spread the filling over the
dough lining the tin and cover
with remaining dough. Seal
edges (see page 97), brush the
top with water, and sprinkle
with caster sugar. Bake in the
pre-set oven for 30-40 minutes.

Norfolk treacle tart

For shortcrust pastry
8 oz plain flour
4 oz butter
2 oz shortening
water (to mix)

For filling
½ lb golden syrup
2 tablespoons black treacle
1 oz butter
little grated lemon rind
2 small eggs (well beaten)
3 tablespoons cream, or
    evaporated milk

8-inch diameter flan ring

Method
First make the shortcrust pastry
and chill it for about 30 minutes.
Then roll it out and line the flan
ring; bake blind.
    Gently warm the syrup, then
add the black treacle: remove
from the heat and add the butter
in small pieces. When butter is
quite melted, add the lemon
rind, beaten eggs and cream
(or evaporated milk). Mix
thoroughly and pour into the
pastry case. Return to the oven
(set at 350°F or Mark 4) and
continue cooking, on the middle
shelf, until the filling is set
(about 15-20 minutes).

Strawberry tartlets

For rich shortcrust pastry
5 oz plain flour
pinch of salt
3 oz butter
1 teaspoon caster sugar
1 egg yolk
1½-2 tablespoons cold water

For filling
8 oz strawberries
redcurrant jelly glaze

Small tartlet tins

Method

Make the rich shortcrust pastry dough and chill. Roll out the dough and line the tartlet tins; bake blind (for about 8 minutes in an oven at 375°F or Mark 5). Allow to cool.

Remove stalks from the strawberries. Warm the redcurrant jelly glaze but do not boil. Brush the cases with the glaze, arrange strawberries in the cases and brush again with the glaze. The amount of glaze should be generous—sufficient to fill the pastry cases and so hold strawberries firmly in place.

Tartelettes coeur à la crème

4 oz quantity of French flan
  pastry

For filling
4 oz Petit Suisse, or Demi-Sel,
  cream cheese
caster sugar (to taste)
2-3 tablespoons double cream
½ lb small ripe strawberries
  (hulled)
½ lb redcurrant jelly

6-8 tartlet tins

Method

Prepare the pastry and chill for 1 hour before rolling out. Set oven at 375°F or Mark 5. Line tartlet tins with the pastry, prick the bottoms with a fork and bake them blind in pre-set oven for 8-10 minutes.

Rub the cream cheese through a small sieve, add sugar to taste and beat in the cream.

When the pastry cases are cold, fill with the cheese-cream mixture and cover with the strawberries. Make a glaze from the redcurrant jelly and brush the warm glaze over the strawberries. Allow to set before serving.

Strawberry flan

4 oz French flan pastry

For filling
½-¾ lb strawberries
½ lb redcurrant jelly

6-inch diameter flan ring

Method
Roll out pastry dough and line the flan ring; bake blind in the oven pre-set at 375°F or Mark 5 for 15-20 minutes.

Hull the strawberries. Prepare the redcurrant glaze by whisking the redcurrant jelly until fairly smooth and rubbing it through a strainer into a pan. Heat jelly gently without stirring until it is clear, then bring to the boil.

When the flan case is cool, fill with the strawberries and brush with the hot glaze; allow it to set before serving.

Linzer torte

For pastry
8 oz plain flour
pinch of salt
cinnamon
4 oz butter
4 oz caster sugar
1 egg
1 egg yolk
grated lemon rind
2½ oz almonds (ground without blanching)

For filling
1 lb fresh raspberries
caster sugar (to sweeten)

To finish
redcurrant glaze

7-inch diameter flan ring

Method
Bring the raspberries to the boil and cook rapidly for 2-3 minutes with sugar to sweeten.

Sift the flour with salt and cinnamon and make a well in the centre. Place the butter, sugar, eggs and lemon rind in this well and sprinkle almonds on the flour. Work these ingredients together into a dough (as for French flan pastry) and leave this in a cool place for 1 hour.

Set the oven at 375°F or Mark 5. Roll out the dough to a thickness of about ¼-½ inch, line the flan ring and fill with the cold raspberry mixture. Put a lattice of pastry across the top and bake in pre-set oven for 20-30 minutes. When the torte has cooled, brush it with warm redcurrant glaze.

Filling the flan case for Linzer torte   *Putting a lattice of pastry on flan*

Rum pie

For shortcrust pastry

6 oz plain flour
3 oz butter
1 oz shortening
1 tablespoon caster sugar
1 egg yolk
1-2 tablespoons water

For filling

8 fl oz milk
¼ nutmeg (grated)
2 eggs (separated)
3 oz caster sugar
pinch of salt
1 teaspoon gelatine (soaked in
   3 teaspoons cold water)
⅛ pint rum

To finish

1 oz plain block chocolate
1 tablespoon water
¼ pint double cream
1 teaspoon rum
1 dessertspoon caster sugar

7-8 inch diameter flan ring

Method

Prepare the shortcrust pastry dough. Line the flan ring with it and bake blind for 20-25 minutes, then set aside to cool.

To prepare the filling: scald the milk with the nutmeg. Beat the egg yolks, sugar and salt together until thick and light in colour, pour on the hot milk and cook in a double saucepan until the mixture coats the back of a spoon. Stir in the soaked gelatine and allow to cool. When the mixture begins to thicken, stir in the rum and, finally, the stiffly whisked egg whites. Pour into the prepared pastry case and put in the refrigerator to set.

Melt the chocolate in the water, set pan aside and allow it to cool. Whip the cream and divide in half. Flavour half with the rum and the other half with the sugar. Mix the rum-flavoured cream with the cold, melted chocolate, cover the top of the pie with the sugared cream and then coat this with the chocolate cream. Chill again in the refrigerator before serving.

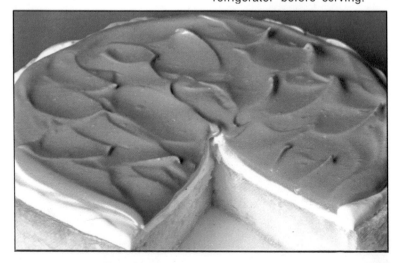

Apricot flan

For rich shortcrust pastry

6 oz plain flour
pinch of salt
4½ oz butter
1 rounded dessertspoon caster
   sugar
1 egg yolk
2 tablespoons water

For filling

1 lb fresh apricots
½ pint water
3 oz granulated sugar
apricot glaze

7-8 inch diameter flan ring

Method

Make the rich shortcrust pastry dough and chill.

Put the water and sugar into a shallow pan, dissolve on a slow heat, then boil rapidly, for 2 minutes; draw syrup aside.

Wash the apricots and cut in half with a serrated-edged, stainless steel knife, or fruit knife, by cutting down to, and round, the stone from the stalk end, following the slight grove on the side of the apricot. Give the fruit a twist to halve it. If the stones do not come away easily, poach the apricots whole. Once cooked the stones can be taken out without breaking the fruit. Some of the stones can be cracked, the kernels skinned and added to the fruit for special flavour.

Place the halved apricots in a pan, cut side uppermost, cover in syrup and heat gently to boiling point. This will draw out the juice and so increase the quantity of syrup, although this will not in the first instance cover the fruit. Simmer for about 15 minutes, or until the apricots are tender. Cool in the syrup.

Roll out the pastry dough, line the flan ring and bake blind. Cool on a pastry rack.

The prepared apricot glaze should be hot and very well reduced. If too thin, reduce to a thicker consistency by boiling the liquid quickly in an uncovered pan. Brush a light coating of glaze over the bottom and sides of the flan. Lift the apricots from the syrup with a spoon and arrange in the flan. Brush well with the hot glaze.

Alternatively, the apricot syrup can be thickened (see page 149) and used in place of jam glaze. Jam is better, however, if the flan has to be kept for a while before serving.

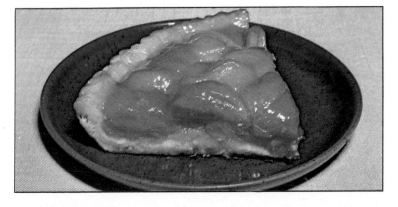

Almond and apricot flan

1 lb fresh apricots
sugar syrup (made with ½ pint
   water and 3 tablespoons
   granulated sugar)
2 tablespoons apricot jam (sieved)
1 rounded teaspoon arrowroot
   (mixed with 1 tablespoon
   water) — optional
¼-½ pint double cream (whipped,
   sweetened with little caster
   sugar and flavoured with kirsch)
few almonds (blanched and split)

For almond pastry

1 oz shortening
3 oz butter
6 oz plain flour
1½ oz ground almonds
1½ oz caster sugar
1 egg yolk
1-2 tablespoons cold water

8-inch diameter flan ring

Method

To make syrup, dissolve sugar
slowly in the water, then boil
rapidly for 2 minutes Halve and
stone apricots (see page 113)
and poach them in the syrup.

Prepare the pastry dough.
Rub the fats into the flour, add
the ground almonds and sugar.
Mix the egg yolk with water and
add to the dry ingredients. Work
lightly to a firm dough and chill
slightly. Roll out, line into flan
ring and bake blind for about
10-15 minutes at 375°F or Mark 5.

Drain the apricots, boil the
juice until thick and syrupy, then
add jam and stir until melted.
Strain, and if glaze is too runny,
thicken with the slaked arrowroot; allow this glaze to cool
before using.

When flan case is quite cold,
fill with whipped cream, arrange
the apricots and almonds on top
and brush with glaze.

*When baked flan case is quite cold,
it is filled with whipped cream*

*Drained apricot halves are carefully
arranged to cover surface of the flan*

The finished flan is brushed with glaze to give it a rich, golden gloss

Beauceronne tart

For rich shortcrust pastry

6 oz plain flour
pinch of salt
4½ oz butter
1 egg yolk
1 rounded dessertspoon caster
    sugar
2 tablespoons cold water

For filling

8 oz curd cheese
2 oz butter
2 rounded tablespoons caster
    sugar
2 rounded tablespoons raisins
2 tablespoons double cream
3 eggs (separated)
2 level tablespoons plain flour

8-inch diameter flan ring, or sand-
wich tin

Method

Make the rich shortcrust pastry
dough and set aside to chill.
Line flan ring or tin with the
dough. Set the oven at 375-400°F
or Mark 5-6.

Sieve the cheese and work
well in a warm bowl. (This will
help the cheese to absorb the
butter, sugar, cream and yolks
without curdling, and allow the
whisked egg whites to be folded
in easily.)

Cream the butter with the
sugar in a bowl and beat well.
Stir in the raisins, cream and
egg yolks. Stir this into cheese,
then, when well mixed, whip
egg whites stiffly and, using a
metal spoon, fold into the mixture with the sifted flour.

Turn into the pastry case and
bake for 35-40 minutes in pre-
set oven.

Leave to cool before turning
out of the tin. Serve cold, with
lightly whipped cream if wished.

Cherry and praline flan

6 oz French flan pastry

For praline filling

4 oz praline
1 tablespoon custard powder
¼ pint milk
¼ pint double cream (whipped)
1 teaspoon caster sugar

For topping

1 can pitted dark, or Morello,
    cherries
1 wineglass red wine
3-4 tablespoons redcurrant jelly
grated rind and juice of 1 orange

8-inch diameter flan ring

Method

Set oven at 375°F or Mark 5.

Mix the custard powder and
milk to a paste in a saucepan
and bring to the boil. Turn into
a basin, whisk well and cover
with wet greaseproof paper to
prevent a skin from forming.

Cooked almonds and sugar being
grated to make praline powder for
the filling

Roll out pastry dough, line the flan ring and bake blind in preset oven for 12-15 minutes.

For topping: drain cherries. Boil wine to reduce it to half its quantity, add redcurrant jelly, orange rind and juice and heat gently until jelly has melted. Mix in cherries (keeping back a few to garnish the top) and leave to cool.

When custard is cold, fold in whipped cream and praline, with caster sugar to taste. Fill pastry case with praline cream and spoon on cherry topping. Arrange reserved cherries round the edge of the flan.

This rich cherry and praline flan makes an unusual sweet for a party meal

Apple flan ménagère

For rich shortcrust pastry
6 oz plain flour
pinch of salt
3 oz butter
1 oz shortening
1 rounded dessertspoon caster
   sugar
1 egg yolk
1-2 tablespoons cold water

For filling
4-5 even-size cooking apples
caster sugar
apricot glaze

7-inch diameter shallow flan ring

This flan should be made in the shallow French flan ring, because if filling is too thick, too much juice runs and makes the bottom pastry soft.

Method
Make the rich shortcrust pastry dough and line the flan ring; pinch round the edge to decorate and chill for 10-15 minutes. Set oven at 375-400°F or Mark 5-6.

Peel and slice apples thinly and place immediately in the flan, arranging top layer neatly in a circle. Dust with caster sugar and bake for 25-30 minutes in pre-set oven, allowing apples to colour. Remove the ring and brush flan with hot apricot glaze.

Watchpoint Only the top layer of apple is dusted with sugar. The glaze at the end provides all the sweetening necessary, even for very sour cooking apples. The sugar on the top layer helps the apple slices to brown, and this looks attractive through the glaze.

Tarte aux pommes à l'orange

4 oz French flan pastry

For filling
2 lb cooking apples
3-4 tablespoons granulated sugar
grated rind of 2 oranges

To finish
2 seedless oranges (sliced in
   rounds)
3-4 tablespoons apricot glaze

7-8 inch diameter flan ring

Method
Set oven at 375°F or Mark 5. Roll out pastry dough and line flan ring. Bake blind in pre-set oven for 15 minutes.

Quarter, core and slice apples into a buttered pan, cover with a tight-fitting lid and cook to a pulp. Rub through a strainer and return purée to the pan with sugar and orange rind. Cook until thick, stirring all the time. Turn out and cool a little.

Fill the flan case with the apple purée and smooth over the top. Cut peel and pith from the oranges, slice into rounds and arrange on top of the flan. Brush the oranges with warm glaze.

Mincemeat flan de luxe

For rich shortcrust pastry
8 oz plain flour
salt
4 oz butter
2 oz lard
1 dessertspoon caster sugar
1 egg yolk
2-3 tablespoons water

For fresh mincemeat
8 oz Cox's apples (weight when
   peeled and cored)
1 oz candied orange peel
8 oz raisins
8 oz currants
4 oz sultanas
6 oz grapes (peeled and pipped)
2 rounded tablespoons almonds
   (blanched and shredded)
grated rind and juice of 1 small
   lemon
pinch of mixed spice
6 oz soft brown sugar
1 oz butter (melted)
1 small glass brandy, or sherry

To decorate
2-3 tablespoons whipped cream
little rum, or brandy

*8-inch diameter flan ring; 3-inch
   diameter plain cutter*

Only half this quantity of mincemeat is needed to fill the 8-inch
flan ring. The remainder will
keep up to 2 weeks in sealed
jars (see method).

Method
Prepare pastry dough and chill
slightly.

To prepare mincemeat: dried
fruit should be washed and
dried, candied peel well soaked
in water to soften. Chop apples
and candied peel separately,
then mix with the other ingredients. If the grapes are large, cut
them into 2-3 pieces.

When mincemeat is well mixed
set aside quantity to be used
immediately and fill remainder
into clean, dry jars. Cover with
circle of greaseproof paper and
cellophane, then tie down or
secure with an elastic band.

Set the flan ring on a baking
sheet. Set oven at 375°F or
Mark 5.

Use three-quarters of the pastry to line the flan ring. Fill with
mincemeat. Roll out the remaining pastry and cut a circle the
same size as the flan ring. Stamp
out a hole in the middle with a
plain cutter. Put this pastry ring
on top of the flan, crimp round
the edge to decorate and seal
(see page 95), brush with water
and sprinkle with caster sugar.
Bake in the pre-set oven for
30-40 minutes.

Just before serving pile 2-3
tablespoons of whipped cream,
lightly flavoured with rum or
brandy, in the middle of the flan.

Below left: After lining flan ring with three-quarters of the pastry, the mince-meat is spooned in. A hole is cut out of the middle of the remaining pastry, which is then laid over top of flan and edges are crimped

Mince pies

about 1½ lb mincemeat
(see page 120)
brandy, or rum, or sherry
caster sugar (for dusting)

For rich shortcrust pastry
8 oz plain flour
pinch of salt
5 oz butter
1 oz shortening, or lard
1 egg yolk
2-3 tablespoons cold water

Pastry cutters, patty tins

This quantity makes about 18 pies approximately 2 inches in diameter.

Method
Make pastry dough and chill well. Set oven at 400°F or Mark 6. On a lightly floured surface, roll out half the dough fairly thinly, and stamp into rounds (size to fit patty tins) with a cutter.

Add trimmings to second half of the dough and roll out a little thinner than first half. Stamp in rounds, a little larger than first.

Mix brandy, rum or sherry with mincemeat. Put larger dough rounds into patty tins, with a good spoonful of mincemeat to fill well. Place smaller rounds on top, pinch edges together, brush lightly with cold water, dust with sugar.

Cook for 15-20 minutes until nicely brown. Cool slightly before taking from tins.

Savoury flans and pies

Flans or pies with savoury fillings make meals in themselves or snacks. The secret is in using plenty of the chosen filling. For deep pies, like the steak and kidney on page 144, use a good, deep pie dish and fill it well up with meat and gravy. For flans, use the 1 inch English flan ring and be as generous with the filling as you can, without spoiling the appearance.

A savoury pastry will suit all sorts of occasions; it will make a main dish for lunch or supper, first course for a dinner party, or the centre piece of a buffet. The smaller vol-au-vents and bouchées are ideal for entertaining when there are too many guests to seat at a table.

Many of the dishes in this section are traditional or regional. None more so than the pizza, which originally was a speciality of Naples. Now an international dish, it typifies many savoury pies in that it was first devised as a way of using up leftovers from other cooking (in this case leftover bread dough, tomato sauce, ham, cheese and other savoury bits).

Many a good pie can be made up by judicious mixing of flavours within a tasty pastry crust and we hope that our special favourites, given here, will encourage you to go on and experiment for yourselves.

Quiche lorraine

For shortcrust pastry
6 oz plain flour
pinch of salt
3 oz butter, or margarine
1 oz shortening
2 tablespoons cold water

For filling
1 egg
1 egg yolk
1 rounded tablespoon grated
   cheese
salt and pepper
¼ pint single cream, or milk
½ oz butter
2-3 rashers of streaky bacon
   (diced)
1 small onion (thinly sliced), or
   12 spring onions

7-inch diameter flan ring

Method
Make the shortcrust pastry and
set aside to chill. Set oven at
375°F or Mark 5.

When chilled, roll out pastry
dough and line the flan ring.
Beat the egg and extra yolk in
a bowl, add the cheese, seasoning and cream or milk. Melt the
butter in a small pan, add the
bacon and sliced onion, or
whole spring onions, and cook
slowly until just golden in
colour. Then turn contents of
the pan into the egg mixture,
mix well and pour into the
pastry case.

Bake for about 25-30 minutes
in pre-set oven.

This egg and bacon tart is a dish from the Lorraine region of France

124

Salé

(Swiss cheese dish)

For rich shortcrust pastry
6 oz plain flour
pinch of salt
3 oz butter
1 oz shortening
1 egg yolk
2 tablespoons cold water

For filling
½ pint béchamel sauce
little double cream
3 eggs
4½ oz Gruyère cheese (grated)
salt and pepper
grated nutmeg

7-inch diameter flan ring

Method
Make the rich shortcrust pastry dough and set aside to chill. When chilled, roll out dough and line the flan ring. Set oven at 375-400°F or Mark 5-6.

Make the béchamel sauce (but add a little cream to it) and when cool beat in the eggs and grated cheese; add plenty of seasoning and a grating of nutmeg. Pour the mixture into the pastry case and bake for about 25 minutes in pre-set oven.

Pissaladière

For rich shortcrust pastry
8 oz plain flour
pinch of salt
4 oz butter
2 oz shortening
1 egg yolk
2 tablespoons cold water

For filling
1 lb onions (thinly sliced)
4 tablespoons olive oil
12-15 black olives (stoned)
2 teaspoons French mustard
6-8 tomatoes (scalded, skinned and thickly sliced)
14 anchovy fillets (split lengthways, soaked in 2-3 tablespoons milk)
mixed herbs (basil, thyme, sage) — chopped
2 oz Gruyère cheese (grated)

7-8 inch diameter flan ring

This flan, with its black olives and anchovy fillets, is characteristic of dishes from Nice in southern France.

Method
Make the rich shortcrust pastry dough, roll out, line the flan ring and chill.

Cook the onions slowly in half the oil for about 20 minutes until golden, and then cool. Set oven at 400°F or Mark 6.

Spread the mustard over the pastry, place the onions evenly on top, then arrange the tomato slices over and cover these with a lattice of anchovy fillets (well drained from the milk), and place a halved olive in each 'window pane'. Sprinkle a few herbs over the top and finish with the grated cheese. Spoon the remaining oil over flan and bake for about 30-35 minutes.

Smoked haddock flan

For shortcrust pastry

6 oz plain flour
pinch of salt
1 oz shortening
3 oz butter
2 tablespoons cold water

For filling

1½ lb smoked haddock
1½-2 lb potatoes (boiled and
   creamed)
1 egg yolk
2 tablespoons grated cheese
1 small bunch of spring onions, or
   green part of 1 leek (shredded,
   well blanched)
2 hard-boiled eggs (quartered)
½ pint béchamel sauce

8-inch diameter flan ring

Method

Make the shortcrust pastry dough and set aside to chill. Roll it out, line flan ring and bake blind for 20 minutes in the oven at 400°F or Mark 6.

Cut fins and tail from haddock, wash, put in a pan with milk to cover and simmer for 7-10 minutes. Then flake fish with a knife.

Add the egg yolk to the creamed potato with 1 rounded tablespoon of grated cheese. Arrange flaked haddock on the pastry with onions on top and quartered eggs round the edge. Spoon the béchamel sauce over all and decorate with creamed potato round the edge and across the centre (preferably using a forcing bag and an 8-cut rose pipe). Sprinkle with the rest of the grated cheese and brown in oven at 400-475°F or Mark 7 if filling is already hot. If filling is cold, heat flan for about 20-30 minutes at 350°F or Mark 4.

White fish flan

For rich shortcrust pastry
6 oz plain flour
pinch of salt
3 oz butter
1 oz shortening
1 egg yolk
1-2 tablespoons water

For filling
1 cup white fish
1 oz butter
1 cup finely sliced onions
1 rounded dessertspoon plain flour
¼ pint milk
salt and pepper
grate of nutmeg
2 eggs (beaten)
3 tomatoes (halved)
grated cheese

7-inch diameter flan ring

Method
Make rich shortcrust pastry dough and chill.

Roll out dough and line flan ring; bake blind. Cool.

To cook fish, poach in water to cover with a little lemon juice, at 350°F or Mark 4, for about 15 minutes. Then flake with a knife.

Heat butter in a pan, add onions and soften; then mix in flour and add milk. Stir until boiling, draw pan aside, add seasoning and a dust of grated nutmeg, together with the beaten eggs.

Scald tomatoes, skin and flick out seeds, then cut in halves. Arrange tomatoes, cut side down, with white fish on bottom of flan, season well and pour over sauce. Scatter grated cheese on top and bake in the oven, at 375°F or Mark 5, for about 20-25 minutes until well set and golden-brown.

Crab flan

8 oz quantity of rich shortcrust pastry (using 4 oz butter and 2 oz shortening)

For filling
1 lb frozen crab meat (½ dark and ½ white meat)
¼ pint thick béchamel sauce
2 oz butter (creamed)
salt and pepper
1-2 tablespoons double cream
1 cucumber
black pepper (ground from mill)
½ pint mayonnaise
2 hard-boiled eggs
chopped parsley

8-9 inch diameter flan ring

Method
Roll out the pastry dough, line the flan ring and bake blind. Set aside to cool.

Work the cold béchamel sauce into dark crab meat, add creamed butter, seasoning and lightly whipped cream.

Finely slice the cucumber, sprinkle with salt between slices and leave them pressed between two plates for 30 minutes; drain and rinse with ice-cold water. Dry cucumber and season with black pepper. Mix the mayonnaise with the white crab meat.

Arrange the dark crab meat and cucumber, then white crab meat, in the flan case. Shred white of the hard-boiled eggs and mix with chopped parsley, sieve yolks and use both to decorate the flan.

Timbale à l'indienne

8 oz quantity of rich shortcrust
   pastry
paprika pepper

For curry sauce

2 small onions
1 oz butter
1 dessertspoon curry powder
béchamel sauce (made with 1 oz
   butter, 1 oz flour, ¾ pint
   flavoured milk)
1-2 tablespoons double cream
salt and pepper (optional)

For filling

6 oz prawns (shelled)
3 hard-boiled eggs (quartered)
3 oz long grain rice (cooked)

Deep 7-8 inch diameter sandwich tin

Method

Line pastry dough into the sandwich tin and bake blind.

Chop onions very finely, cook them in butter until soft but not coloured, then add curry powder and cook for 3-4 minutes. Add the béchamel sauce and simmer for 2-3 minutes, then add the cream, and season if necessary.

Fill pastry case with alternate layers of prawns, eggs and rice, and the sauce, piling up the mixture well. Arrange a few prawns on the top and dust with paprika pepper; hand any remaining sauce separately.

Timbale à l'indienne, with a substantial filling of prawns, eggs and rice

Mushroom flan

For shortcrust pastry

6 oz plain flour
pinch of salt
2 oz butter
2 oz shortening
2 tablespoons cold water

For filling

½ pint milk
1 blade of mace
1 bayleaf
6 peppercorns
1½ oz butter
1 medium-size onion (thinly sliced)
6 oz mushrooms (sliced)
3 tablespoons plain flour
2 tablespoons double cream (optional)
1 egg yolk
salt and pepper
1 small egg (for glazing)

7-inch diameter flan ring

Method

Make the shortcrust pastry dough, roll out and line the flan ring, reserving about one-third to cut into strips for the top. Set aside to chill. Set oven at 400°F or Mark 6.

Infuse the milk with the mace, bayleaf and peppercorns until well flavoured; then strain off into a jug. Scrape (using a plastic scraper) or rinse out the pan, melt half the butter in the same pan and add the onion. Cook slowly until soft but without browning, then add the mushrooms and increase the heat. Cook briskly for 2-3 minutes, stirring occasionally. Then draw off the heat, add the rest of the butter and stir in the flour. Add the milk by degrees, blend thoroughly, and stir over heat until boiling. Draw aside again, to add the cream, egg yolk and seasoning. Turn on to a plate to cool.

Fill the flan with this mixture. Roll out the remaining pastry dough and cut into thin strips. Lay a diagonal lattice over the top of the flan, pressing the ends of the strips well down on to the edge. Cover this with a strip of pastry to neaten. Beat the small egg with salt and brush over the flan. Bake for 25-35 minutes in pre-set oven.

Salmon Koulibiac

12 oz quantity of puff pastry
egg wash
sprigs of watercress
½ pint mock hollandaise sauce

For filling
1 lb fresh salmon (poached)
salt and pepper
lemon juice
¼ lb mushrooms
6 spring onions
2-3 oz butter
2 eggs (hard-boiled)
6 oz long grain rice (boiled)

Method

Remove the skin and bones from poached salmon and flake into a bowl; season with salt, pepper and lemon juice. Wash the mushrooms in salted water, dry and slice them. Trim and chop the spring onions and put in a pan with half the butter; cook them slowly for 1 minute, then add the mushrooms and simmer for 5 minutes. Melt the remaining butter. Chop the eggs and add them to the salmon with the rice, mushroom mixture and remaining melted butter. Taste for seasoning.

Set oven at 400°F or Mark 6. Roll out puff pastry dough into a rectangle, cut off a 1-inch wide strip for fleurons (crescent shapes); cut off two-thirds of the remaining dough, put the salmon mixture on this larger piece and fold the dough around it. Lay the other piece of dough over the top, seal edges, brush with egg wash and decorate with fleurons, bake in pre-set oven for about 25-30 minutes. Garnish with watercress and serve mock hollandaise sauce separately.

Seafood flan

6 oz quantity of flaky, or puff, pastry
½-¾ lb mixed shellfish (eg. prawns, scallops and mussels)
¼ lb button mushrooms (sliced)
½ oz butter
1 green pepper (blanched, seeds and core removed, and shredded)
1 egg (beaten)

For sauce
1 shallot (chopped)
1 oz butter
1 teaspoon curry powder
1 oz plain flour
scant ¾ pint milk
salt and pepper
2 tablespoons double cream

Deep 8-inch diameter pie plate, or 9-inch long pie dish

Method

First prepare filling: sauté mushrooms in ½ oz butter. Prepare the shellfish; if using scallops or mussels have them previously cooked and the prawns shelled or carefully thawed out. Mix shellfish with green pepper and mushrooms.

Soften shallot in the butter, add curry powder and, after 1 minute, stir in the flour. Pour on milk, blend, then stir until boiling. Season and finish with the cream. Pour sauce over the shellfish, mix together carefully and turn into the pie plate or dish. Roll out pastry to a thickness of ¼-½ inch and chill for 10-15 minutes. Set oven at 400°F or Mark 6.

When mixture is cold, cover with pastry; decorate and brush with beaten egg. Bake in pre-set oven for 25-30 minutes or until well browned, then serve.

Prawn gougère

choux pastry for 3-4 people
2 oz Cheddar cheese (diced)
salt and pepper

For filling

8 oz prawns (shelled)
1 medium-size onion
½ oz butter
1 dessertspoon plain flour
½ pint stock, or milk
1 teaspoon chopped parsley
2 tomatoes (skinned, seeds
  removed, and shredded)
chopped parsley (to garnish)
1 tablespoon finely grated
  Parmesan cheese
1 tablespoon browned crumbs

*Deep 8-inch diameter pie plate, or
ovenproof dish, or 6 small individual cocottes*

Gougère is a savoury choux pastry dish mixed with cheese and served plain, or with a savoury filling.

Shellfish
Shellfish need careful preparation, and must be eaten very fresh. Full instructions for preparing mussels and scallops are given on page 154.

Method

Prepare the choux pastry, stirring in cheese and seasoning after beating in the egg.

To prepare filling: slice the onion and cook it slowly in the butter until soft. Draw the pan aside, stir in the flour and pour in the stock (or milk), stir until boiling.

Take pan off the heat and add the prawns, parsley and shredded tomatoes. Set oven at 400°F or Mark 6. Well butter the pie plate (or ovenproof dish or cocottes), arrange the choux pastry around the sides, hollowing out the centre. Pour the filling into this, dust with grated cheese and crumbs mixed together. Bake in pre-set moderately hot oven for 30-40 minutes (or 15-20 minutes for individual cocottes). When choux is well risen and evenly browned, take gougère out of oven and sprinkle well with the chopped parsley before serving.

Gougère with chicken livers, game, or ham

choux pastry for 3-4 people
2 oz Cheddar cheese (diced)
salt and pepper

For filling
1 oz butter
2 chicken livers, or 4 oz cooked
    game, or ham (shredded)
1 medium-size onion (sliced, or
    chopped)
1 large mushroom (sliced)
1 dessertspoon plain flour
¼ pint stock
1 tomato (skinned, deseeded and
    quartered)
1 tablespoon finely grated
    Parmesan cheese
1 tablespoon browned crumbs
1 teaspoon chopped parsley

Pie plate, or ovenproof dish

Method
Prepare choux pastry, stirring in cheese after the beaten eggs. Season.

Melt half the butter in a pan, and if using liver add it now; sauté briskly on all sides for about 3 minutes. Remove liver from pan. Soften onion slowly in the remaining butter, then add mushroom and cook for 2 minutes. Draw pan aside, blend in flour and stock and simmer for about 5 minutes. Take pan off the heat and add liver, or game or ham, and tomatoes.

Set oven at 400°F or Mark 6.

Well grease the pie plate, or ovenproof dish. Arrange choux pastry around the sides, leaving a hollow in the centre. Pour the filling into this and dust with grated cheese mixed with the browned crumbs.

Bake in pre-set oven for 30-40 minutes until gougère is well risen and brown. Sprinkle with parsley before serving.

Pizza

Basic pizza dough

1 lb plain flour
1 teaspoon salt
1 oz fresh yeast
2 teaspoons caster sugar
about ¼ pint milk (warmed)
3-4 eggs (beaten)
4 oz butter (creamed)

Method

Sift the flour and salt into a warmed basin. Cream yeast and sugar and add to the warmed milk with the beaten eggs: add this liquid to the flour and beat thoroughly. Work the creamed butter into the dough. Cover and leave for 40 minutes to rise. **Note:** for the best pizza, it is wise to use a flan ring to keep the dough in position. It has the added advantage of enabling you to cover the entire surface with topping without it running over and sticking to your baking sheet.

Flour the dough lightly and put it out with the palm of your hand on a floured baking sheet to the size of the flan ring. Then place greased flan ring round it. Arrange topping. Prove pizza for 10-15 minutes, until dough begins to swell (i.e. put in a warm place such as over the stove or in a warming drawer at about 80-85°F), then bake in pre-set oven for 30-35 minutes. Lift off flan ring and slide pizza on to a bread board or wooden platter to serve.

Patting out the pizza dough to the size of the flan ring

Yeast. The quantity given in this recipe is for fresh yeast. Dried yeast may be used instead, but the quantity should be adjusted according to the manufacturer's instructions.

The name **Pizza** originated from the area around Naples. It is not certain, however, that the nearby village of Pizza, where the flour for the best pizza dough is grown and ground, can claim to be its creator. A pizza may first have been made to use up left-over bread dough and tomato sauce, plus whatever sausage, ham or cheese happened to be available.

Haddock and mushroom pizza

¼ quantity of basic dough

For topping
1 lb smoked haddock
béchamel sauce (made with 1 oz
  plain flour, 1 oz butter, ¼ pint
  flavoured milk)
1 oz butter
1 shallot (finely chopped)
6 oz mushrooms (quartered)
salt and pepper

8-inch diameter flan ring

Method
Cover the smoked haddock with water, bring it slowly to the boil; cover, turn off heat and leave for 10 minutes.

Meanwhile make béchamel sauce.

Remove skin and bones from the haddock and flake flesh carefully. Melt 1 oz butter, add shallot, cook for 2-3 minutes, then add quartered mushrooms and sauté briskly for 2-3 minutes. Add béchamel sauce and haddock; season to taste.

Set oven at 400°F or Mark 6. Pat out the dough, cover with topping, prove and bake in pre-set oven.

Pizza Cordon Bleu

¼ quantity of basic dough

For topping
2 shallots (finely chopped)
1 wineglass white wine
1 lb scampi
4 oz mushrooms (chopped)
1 oz butter
¾ oz plain flour
1 clove of garlic (crushed with
  ½ teaspoon salt)
¼ pint chicken stock
1 teaspoon tomato purée
4 tomatoes
salt and pepper

8-inch diameter flan ring

Method
Simmer shallot in wine until wine is reduced to half the quantity. Add scampi and mushrooms and cook very slowly for 5 minutes; set pan aside.

Melt butter, add flour and when coloured add the garlic, stock and tomato purée, stir until boiling, then cook for 3-4 minutes. Scald tomatoes, skin, quarter, and remove seeds, cut flesh into strips. Add scampi mixture to tomatoes and sauce. Season to taste.

Set oven at 400°F or Mark 6. Pat out the dough and cover with the topping; prove and bake in pre-set oven.

Ham pizza

¼ quantity of basic dough (see page 134)

For topping
2 oz butter
1 large Spanish onion (about ½ lb) — finely sliced
6 oz ham (shredded)
2 oz mortadella sausage (shredded)
2-3 tablespoons mango, or tomato, chutney

Method
Melt butter, add onion and cook slowly until very brown. Add shredded ham and mortadella, moisten with chutney.

Set oven at 400°F or Mark 6. Pat out the dough, cover with the topping, prove and bake in pre-set oven.

Spooning the prepared ham topping on to the pizza dough

Pizza napolitana

¼ quantity of basic dough (see page 134)

For topping
4-6 anchovy fillets
2 tablespoons milk
1 lb ripe tomatoes
1-2 tablespoons olive oil
1 small onion (finely chopped)
1 dessertspoon chopped marjoram, or basil
salt and pepper
4 oz Bel Paese, or Mozzarella, cheese (sliced)

8-inch diameter flan ring

Method
Split the anchovy fillets in two lengthways and soak them in the milk; set aside.

Scald and skin the tomatoes, cut away the hard core, squeeze gently to remove seeds, then slice. Heat the oil in a frying pan; add chopped onion and, after a few minutes, the sliced tomatoes. Draw pan aside and add the herbs; season well.

Set oven at 400°F or Mark 6. Cover dough with tomato mixture, place cheese slices on this and arrange anchovies lattice-wise over the top. Prove pizza, then bake in pre-set oven for 30-35 minutes.

Pizzas are popular party dishes. Choose from several different fillings: smoked haddock and mushroom (at back), ham (centre), napolitana (front left) and Cordon Bleu (front right)

Puff pastry flan case

8 oz puff pastry
egg wash

Two pan lids, or rings (8-inch and 6-inch diameter)

Method

Set oven at 425°F or Mark 7. Roll out puff pastry, a scant ½ inch thick.

To cut flan case: cut out a round with larger lid, keeping a straight edge. With smaller lid cut out a centre circle. You will then have one outer ring (1 inch wide) and one large round (6 inches in diameter).

Slide this outer ring to one side and re-roll 6-inch round with any trimmings to make a larger but thinner round (about ¼ inch thick and 8 inches in diameter) to form flan base.

Lift this round of pastry on to the damp baking sheet, brush very lightly with egg wash, then lift the ring on to it. Neaten both layers into a perfect round and cut away any surplus pastry. Brush top of the ring with egg wash and mark with the back of a knife in diagonal lines to decorate.

Prick the centre with a fork, chill for 10-15 minutes in refrigerator, then bake in pre-set oven for 25-30 minutes. Cool slightly before sliding off baking sheet. The flan case is now ready for a savoury or sweet filling (see shortcrust pastry flans, pages 105-129).

Bouchées

12 oz puff pastry (well chilled)
egg wash

2½-inch diameter fluted cutter, 1½-inch diameter cutter (fluted or plain)

Method

Set oven at 425°F or Mark 7. Roll out pastry, not more than ½ inch thick.

To cut bouchées: stamp out rounds with larger fluted cutter. Lift rounds on to a dampened baking sheet.

Lightly brush rounds with egg wash and with smaller cutter mark the centre of each one (for lid). To save time, brush whole sheet of pastry with egg wash before cutting out bouchées.

Chill bouchées for a few minutes, then bake in pre-set oven for 15-20 minutes or until golden-brown. Lift on to a rack to cool. With the point of a small knife lift out centre lid and scoop out any soft centre. Insert a good tablespoon of filling (see pages 140, 141) and replace top.

Watchpoint The larger the case, the thicker the pastry must be rolled. A vol-au-vent of 6-7 inch diameter calls for a ½-¾ inch thickness of pastry, whereas a bouchée of 1½-2 inch diameter needs a ¼-inch thickness of pastry. If pastry is too thick for the size of bouchée, it will topple over in oven when it has risen to a certain height.

However good pastry is, some shrinkage in baking has to be allowed for. When choosing a cutter take one a size larger than you want for your bouchée: a 2½-inch round of uncooked pastry will make a 2¼-inch bouchée.

Vol-au-vent

8 oz puff pastry (well chilled)
egg wash

Pan lid (6-7 inch diameter), 3-4 inch
diameter plain cutter

Method

Set oven at 425°F or Mark 7. Roll out the puff pastry on a floured slab or work top to a square, ½-¾ inch thick.

To cut vol-au-vent shape: place pan lid on pastry and cut round it with a knife; hold the knife slantwise to form a bevelled edge, wider at the base. Turn this round of pastry upside down on to a dampened baking sheet, so that the widest part is on top. Brush lightly with the egg wash.

Watchpoint Egg wash acts as a seal, so don't let it touch the cut edge or it will stop the pastry from rising.

With the cutter (or a small pan lid), mark a circle in the centre of round with the back of a knife and mark lines for decoration. Chill pastry 10-15 minutes if it seems a little soft, then bake in pre-set oven for 25-30 minutes.

When well risen and a good colour, slide on to a rack to cool. While still warm cut round the circular mark with the point of a small knife to remove the top. Set this aside and carefully scoop out some of the soft centre. Place vol-au-vent case on serving dish before filling. (It can be baked beforehand but do not add filling until just before serving.)

1 *Make a vol-au-vent shape by placing a pan lid on the rolled out pastry and cutting round it*
2 *Place pastry underside up on baking sheet; mark out centre circle and lines for decoration*
3 *When cooked, cut out the centre circle and scoop out some of soft vol-au-vent centre. The case is then ready for filling*

Fillings for bouchées and vol-au-vents

Vol-au-vents can be filled with shellfish, veal, chicken, sweetbreads and mushrooms, bound with a white or velouté sauce (see recipes on pages 141 and 142).

Velouté sauce

¾ oz butter
1 rounded tablespoon plain flour
⅓-½ pint stock
2½ fl oz top of milk
salt and pepper
squeeze of lemon juice

For liaison (optional)
1 egg yolk (lightly beaten)
2 tablespoons cream

This sauce is made with a blond roux, at which point liquid is added. This is well-flavoured stock (made from veal, chicken or fish bones, according to dish with which sauce is being served), or liquid in which food was simmered or poached.

Method

Melt butter in a saucepan, stir in flour and cook for about 5 seconds. When roux is colour of pale straw (blond roux) draw pan aside and cool slightly before pouring on stock.

Blend, return to heat and stir until thick. Add top of milk, season and bring to boil. Cook for 4-5 minutes when sauce should be a syrupy consistency. If using a liaison, prepare by mixing egg yolk and cream together and then stir into sauce. Add lemon juice. Remove pan from heat.

Watchpoint Be careful not to let sauce boil after liaison has been added, otherwise the mixture will curdle.

Prawn and egg bouchées

8 oz puff pastry
egg wash

For filling
½ pint béchamel sauce
salt and pepper
2 tablespoons double cream
(optional)
4-6 oz prawns (shelled and
chopped)
2 hard-boiled eggs (finely
chopped)

2½-inch diameter cutter; ½-¾
inch diameter cutter

This quantity fills 8 bouchées,
2-2¼ inches in diameter.

Method

Set oven at 425°F or Mark 7.
Make bouchées as instructed
on page 138. Bake in pre-set
oven for 15-20 minutes until
golden-brown.

To prepare filling: make the
béchamel sauce and simmer for
1-2 minutes. Add a small pinch
of salt, a good pinch of pepper
and cream. Chop prawns a little
and stir into sauce with eggs.

Remove lids and fill bouchées
with mixture. Replace the lids,
reheat for a few minutes in the
oven, then dish up and serve
very hot.

Sweetbread vol-au-vent

8 oz puff pastry
egg wash

For filling:
1 lb lambs sweetbreads
good pinch of salt
slice of lemon
bouquet garni
1 small onion (quartered)
½-¾ pint stock, or water
4 oz button mushrooms
½ oz butter

For sauce
1¼ oz butter
1 rounded tablespoon plain flour
¼ pint creamy milk
salt and pepper
1 egg yolk
1 dessertspoon chopped parsley
squeeze of lemon juice

Method

Soak the sweetbreads for at least 1 hour in cold water. Drain. Put sweetbreads in pan and cover with cold water, add salt and slice of lemon. Bring to the boil, drain and rinse sweetbreads with cold water. Drain, press between two plates with a weight on top. Leave until cold.

Trim any gristle or ducts from sweetbreads, put them into a pan with bouquet garni, onion and enough stock or water to cover; simmer for 10 minutes, or until tender. Put all in a bowl, remove bouquet garni and onion. Pour stock back into pan and reduce to ¾ cup. Pour into a dish, set aside. Sauté mushrooms in butter, set aside.

Set oven at 425°F or Mark 7.

Roll out pastry dough, cut out vol-au-vent (see page 139), brush with egg wash. Mark diagonal lines round edge. Bake in pre-set oven for 25-30 minutes, or until well risen and golden-brown.

Prepare sauce: melt butter in a pan, stir in flour, cook for a few seconds, then draw aside and cool. Blend in stock from sweetbreads and milk (reserve 2 tablespoons). Stir sauce until boiling, season.

Mix reserved milk with egg yolk, blend into sauce off heat, add parsley with lemon juice. Add sweetbreads with sauté mushrooms, shake pan gently to mix. Reheat but do not boil.

Take lid off vol-au-vent, scoop out centre, then set on serving dish, fill with sweetbread mixture. Replace lid, slanting it a little, and serve hot.

Veal and ham pie

8 oz flaky pastry (well chilled)
1½ lb veal pie meat, or a piece of oyster (shoulder cut)
1 dessertspoon finely chopped onion
1 dessertspoon finely chopped parsley
grated rind of ¼ lemon
4 oz lean cooked ham, or gammon rasher
3 hard-boiled eggs (quartered)
salt and pepper
¾ pint jellied stock (well seasoned)
egg wash

9-inch diameter pie dish

Method

Set oven at 425°F or Mark 7. Cut the veal in pieces 1-1½ inches square. Mix chopped onion, parsley and lemon rind together and roll meat in this mixture. Shred the ham; or if a gammon rasher is used, cut off the rind and rust, cut in strips and blanch by putting into boiling water and boiling for ½ minute before draining.

Arrange the meat, ham and quartered eggs in layers till the pie dish is full, doming the top slightly. Season. Pour in stock and three-quarters fill the dish.

Roll out the pastry dough, cut a strip to cover the edge of the pie dish, press it down well and then brush with water. Lift the rest of the dough on to the rolling pin and lay it carefully over the dish. Trim round the edge and seal edges with the back of a knife. This separates the layers so that the pastry puffs up during cooking.

Roll out pastry trimmings and cut leaves for decoration. Make a hole in the centre of the pie with the point of a knife and arrange a decoration around this. The hole will allow steam to escape.

Brush with egg wash. Bake for 30 minutes in pre-set oven, then wrap a piece of doubled grease-proof paper over and around the pie, reduce temperature to 350°F or Mark 4 and cook for 1 hour.

1 *Roll out pastry dough to shape of dish, then cut off a strip to cover its edge; press down well, then brush with cold water*
2 *Lift rest of dough on to rolling pin; lay it over pie dish*

Steak and kidney pie

8 oz flaky pastry
egg wash

For filling
1½ lb skirt, or sticking, of beef
6 oz ox kidney
salt and pepper
1 tablespoon plain flour
1 shallot, or ½ small onion (finely chopped)
1 teaspoon chopped parsley (optional)
½ pint cold water, or stock
hot water, or stock (to dilute gravy)

10-inch pie dish, pie funnel

Method

Prepare the flaky pastry dough. Well grease the pie dish. Set oven at 425°F or Mark 7.

Cut the steak into 1-inch cubes; skin and core kidney and cut into pieces; roll both well in seasoned flour (for this amount of meat add as much salt as you can hold between two fingers and your thumb, and half as much pepper, to the 1 tablespoon of flour).

Place meat in the pie dish, sprinkling each layer with the shallot and parsley, and set the pie funnel in the centre. Pour in the cold water or stock and cover pie with the pastry in the following way.

Roll out prepared pastry dough ¼ inch thick and cut off a piece large enough to cover and overlap the top of the pie dish; roll the remainder a little thinner and cut two strips, each ½ inch wide. Damp the edge of the pie dish, press on the strips of pastry and brush with water. Lift the sheet of pastry on your rolling pin and cover the prepared pie.

Watchpoint Do not stretch dough when covering pie or it will shrink during cooking and slide into the pie dish. When trimming the pastry to fit the dish, lift the pie on one hand and, holding a knife at an angle away from the dish, cut the overlapping pastry in short brisk strokes. To trim in one continuous cut would drag the dough, spoil the appearance and prevent it rising in good flakes.

Seal the edges of the double thickness of dough. Scallop the edge (see page 97). Any remaining strips or trimmings of pastry can be used to cut a centre decoration of a rose or thistle, and leaves.

Brush egg wash over top of pie. Arrange the centre decoration, brush pastry with the beaten egg and salt.

Bake 20-30 minutes in the pre-set oven, then cover the pie with a large sheet of damp greaseproof paper, pleating and twisting it under the dish to hold it in place. This prevents the pastry getting too brown and hard during the long cooking which follows. Reduce the oven heat to 325°F or Mark 3 and cook for a further 1½ hours.

To serve: as the gravy in the pie is very strong and concentrated, have ready a small jug of hot stock or water, and when the first portion of pastry is cut, pour in a little to dilute and increase the quantity of gravy for serving.

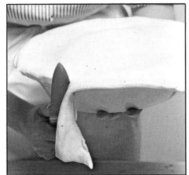

To trim off excess dough, lift pie on one hand. Hold knife at an angle away from dish and use short, brisk strokes (not one continuous cut which would drag the dough and prevent it from rising in good, even flakes)

Raised pork pie

1 lb pork (diced lean and fat)
salt and pepper
1 rounded teaspoon mixed dried
  herbs
¼ pint jellied stock (made from
  pork bones)

For hot water crust

1 lb plain flour
1 teaspoon salt
7 oz lard
¾ pint milk and water (mixed in
  equal proportions)
milk (for glaze)

1 jar (eg. Kilner jar)

Method
Season pork well and add herbs.
Set oven at 350°F or Mark 4.
 Warm a mixing bowl and sift
in flour and salt, make a well in
the centre of the flour. Heat lard
in milk and water. When just
boiling, pour into the well in
the flour, stir quickly with a
wooden spoon until thick, then
work with the hand to a dough.
Turn on to a board, cut off a
quarter of the dough, put it
back in the warm bowl and
cover with a cloth.
 Pat out the rest of dough with
the fist to a thick round, set a
large jar in the centre and work
dough up sides. Let dough cool
then gently lift out jar. Fill
dough case with meat mixture.
Roll or pat out remaining dough
to form a lid, leave a small hole
in it, then put on top of pie,
seal edges. Glaze with milk.
 Slide pie on to a baking sheet
and bake in pre-set oven for
1-1½ hours. If pie is getting too
brown, cover with damp greaseproof paper towards end of
cooking time. When cool, place
a funnel in hole in lid and fill
with jellied stock.

Chicken pie
à la king

8 oz quantity of rough puff, or
  flaky, or puff, pastry
12 oz-1 lb shredded meat of
  1 boiled chicken (about 2-2½ lb)
1-2 green peppers (according to
  size)
2 oz button mushrooms
½ oz butter
1 egg (beaten)

For sauce

1 oz butter
1 oz plain flour
1-1½ pint chicken liquor
2-3 tablespoons double cream

*Deep 8½-inch diameter ovenproof
pie plate, or pie dish*

Method
Prepare the pastry and set aside
in a cool place. Shred the
peppers and blanch for 2-3
minutes in boiling salted water,
then drain. Wash and wipe the
mushrooms, cut in quarters, and
sauté in ½ oz butter for 2-3
minutes, then set aside.
 To make the sauce: melt the
butter, add the flour, and cook
slowly until it is straw-coloured.
Tip on the liquor (in which the
chicken was cooked), stir until
boiling, add the cream and
cook rapidly until of syrupy
consistency. Draw pan aside,
add chicken, peppers and
mushrooms; leave it to cool.
 Turn chicken mixture into pie
plate or dish, cover with pastry,
decorate and brush with beaten
egg. Bake in oven at 400°F or
Mark 7 for 25-35 minutes.

Appendix

Notes and basic recipes

Apple marmelade

When cold, this marmelade (not to be confused with marmalade) sets firmly and is used to fill pastries.

Wash cooking apples, quarter and core. Rub ½ oz butter over sides and bottom of a large pan. Slice apples into pan, add a strip of lemon rind, cover with buttered paper and a lid and cook gently until soft. Stir occasionally. Rub through a sieve or strainer.

Rinse out pan, return purée to it and add sugar to sweeten. Allow 4 oz granulated sugar to 1 pint purée. Cook rapidly, stirring all the time, until mixture is of dropping consistency.

Butter cream 1

2 oz granulated sugar
4 tablespoons water
2 egg yolks
6 oz unsalted butter

For flavourings (optional)
chocolate
coffee essence
zest of orange, or lemon, rind

Method
Dissolve the sugar in water in a saucepan over gentle heat, then boil it steadily until the syrup forms a slim 'thread' between the finger and thumb (216-218°F on a sugar thermometer).
Watchpoint To test between the finger and thumb, remove a little syrup from the pan, off the heat, with the handle of a teaspoon; cool it and then test.

When bubbles subside, pour the syrup on to the egg yolks and whisk until mixture is thick and mousse-like. Cream the butter until soft and add the egg mousse gradually. Flavour to taste with melted sweetened chocolate, or coffee essence, or the zest of orange or lemon rind and use as required.

Butter cream 2

2 egg whites
4 oz icing sugar
8 oz unsalted butter

This butter cream is particularly suitable for tinting to pastel shades.

Method
Whisk the egg whites and icing sugar in a basin over a pan of simmering water until the mixture holds its shape. Cream the butter until soft, then add the meringue mixture to it, a little at a time. Flavour as for butter cream 1, colour and use as required.

Chocolate caraque

Grate 3 oz plain chocolate or chocolate couverture (cooking chocolate). Melt on a plate over hot water and work with a palette knife until smooth. Spread this thinly on a marble slab or laminated surface and leave until nearly set. Then, using a long sharp knife, shave it off the slab, slantwise, using a slight sawing movement and holding the knife almost upright. The chocolate will form long scrolls or flakes. These will keep in an airtight tin but look better when they are freshly made.

Frangipane

4 oz butter
4 oz caster sugar
2 eggs
4 oz ground almonds
1 oz plain flour
orange flower water, or lemon juice, or kirsch, or vanilla essence (to flavour)

Use this recipe for pâtisseries and gâteaux, or as a plain cake.

Method

Soften the butter with a wooden spoon, add the sugar and beat together until light and fluffy. Beat in the eggs gradually, then stir in the almonds and flour. Flavour and use as required.

Glazes

Thickened fruit juice glaze

This is made from the juice of the cooked or canned fruit. To ½ pint of juice take 1 heaped teaspoon of arrowroot and slake (mix) it with 1 tablespoon of the juice. Dissolve 1 tablespoon of red or yellow jam in the rest of the juice and bring to the boil in a saucepan. Then draw aside and add the moistened arrowroot, stir well, return to the heat and bring to the boil. Strain this mixture and, when cool, brush lavishly over the flan.

Apricot glaze

For use with all yellow fruit. Make a pound or so at a time as it keeps well. Store in a covered jar.

Turn the apricot jam into a saucepan, add the juice of ½ lemon and 4 tablespoons water per lb. Bring slowly to the boil and simmer for 5 minutes. Strain and return to the pan. Boil for a further 5 minutes and turn into a jam jar for keeping. If for immediate use, continue boiling until thick, then brush amply over the fruit. If using a smooth jam (with no lumps of fruit), water is not needed.

Redcurrant jelly glaze

For use with all red fruit. Home-made redcurrant jelly (see page 152) is best as it gives the right sharpness of flavour to the fresh fruit. Beat the jelly with a fork or small whisk until it liquefies, then rub through a strainer into a small saucepan. Heat gently without stirring until quite clear (boiling will spoil both colour and flavour). When brushing this glaze over the fruit use a very soft brush. Always work from the centre outwards, drawing the brush, well laden with the glaze, towards the edge.

Gold leaf

This is sold in the form of small books and is comparatively inexpensive; being pure gold it is perfectly harmless to eat. Gold leaf was a favourite form of decoration in Victorian and Edwardian days, not only for cold consommé but also for jellies.

Readers in Great Britain can obtain gold leaf by mail order, or in person, from: George Whiley Ltd., Victoria Road, South Ruislip, Middx.

Icings

Fondant icing

1 lb lump sugar
8 tablespoons water
pinch of cream of tartar

A sugar thermometer is essential for this recipe.

You can now buy blocks or packets of powder of fondant icing. Simply follow the manufacturer's instructions.

Method

Place the sugar and water in a saucepan and dissolve without stirring over a low heat. Using a brush dipped in cold water, wipe round pan at level of the syrup to prevent a crust forming. Add the cream of tartar (dissolved in 1 teaspoon of water), place the lid on the pan, increase the heat and bring to the boil.

Remove the lid after 2 minutes, put a sugar thermometer in and boil the syrup steadily to 240°F. When it has reached this temperature take the pan off the heat at once, wait for the bubbles to subside then pour the mixture very slowly on to a damp marble or laminated plastic slab. Work with a wooden spatula until it becomes a firm and white fondant. Take a small piece of fondant at a time and knead with the finger-tips until smooth.

For storing, pack fondant icing in an airtight jar or tin. When you want to use it, gently warm the fondant with a little sugar syrup to make a smooth cream. The icing should then flow easily. Flavour and colour it just before use with vanilla, lemon, etc. Spread over cake with a palette knife.

Glacé icing

4-5 tablespoons granulated sugar
¼ pint water
8-12 oz icing sugar (finely sifted)
flavouring essence and colouring (as required)

Method
Make sugar syrup by dissolving sugar in ¼ pint of water in a small saucepan. Bring to the boil, and boil steadily for 10 minutes. Remove pan from the heat and when quite cold, add the icing sugar, 1 table-spoon at a time, and beat thoroughly with a wooden spatula. The icing should coat back of spoon and look very glossy. Warm the pan gently on a very low heat.
Watchpoint The pan must not get too hot. You should be able to touch the bottom with the palm of your hand.
Flavour and colour icing; spread over cake with palette knife.

Colouring and flavouring icing

You should use edible colouring for icing. Take great care when adding a colour because one drop too many can change a subtle shading into a gaudy one. A skewer dipped in the bottle of colouring is the best method of adding a colour. From one bowl of icing, you can have five colour changes: from white to yellow, to pink or green, to coffee, to chocolate.

Flavourings are varied but are not meant to overpower and spoil the taste of the cake. You can buy several flavouring essences but you can also make them: strained orange or lemon fruit juice; coffee powder dissolved in a little water; melted chocolate, or cocoa blended with water.

To improve the whiteness of royal icing, add a tiny spot of blue colouring on the point of a skewer and beat it in very thoroughly; too much blue gives icing a greyish tint. Also, 1-2 teaspoons of glycerine added to royal icing will prevent it from becoming excessively hard, and a squeeze of lemon juice added helps to counteract its sweetness.

Meringue cuite

8½ oz icing sugar
4 egg whites

Method
Sift the icing sugar through a fine sieve and tip it into a basin containing beaten egg whites. Place the basin over a pan of simmering water and whisk the whites and sugar together until thick and holding their shape.

Flavour the meringue and use according to recipe.

Nuts

To brown hazelnuts (already shelled) do not blanch first but bake for 7-8 minutes in a moderate oven at 350°F or Mark 4, then rub briskly in a rough cloth to remove skin.

Almonds: buy them with their skins on. This way they retain their oil better. Blanching to remove the skins gives extra juiciness.

To blanch almonds: pour boiling water over the shelled nuts, cover the pan and leave until cool. Then the skins can be easily removed (test one with finger and thumb). Drain, rinse in cold water; press skins off with fingers. Rinse, dry thoroughly.

To brown almonds: blanch, and bake as for hazelnuts (above).

To chop almonds: first blanch, skin, chop and then brown them in the oven, if desired.

To shred almonds: first blanch, skin, split in two and cut each half lengthways in fine pieces. These can then be used as they are or browned quickly in the oven, with or without a sprinkling of caster sugar.

To flake almonds: first blanch and skin, then cut horizontally into flakes with a small sharp knife.

To grind almonds: first blanch, then skin, chop and pound into a paste (use a pestle and mortar, or a grinder, or the butt end of a rolling pin). Home-prepared ground almonds taste much better than the ready-ground variety.

To blanch pistachio nuts: treat as for almonds, but add a pinch of bicarbonate of soda to the water to preserve the colour of the nuts.

Pastry cream

1 egg (separated)
1 egg yolk
2 oz caster sugar
¾ oz flour
½ oz cornflour
½ pint milk

For flavouring (optional)
1 vanilla pod
2-3 oz plain chocolate
1-1½ tablespoons coffee essence

This recipe gives a firm cream that holds its shape and is suitable for filling all types of pâtisseries. This recipe makes about ½ pint.

Method
Cream the two egg yolks and sugar together until white, add the flours and a little of the cold milk to make a smooth paste. Scald the remaining milk with the vanilla pod, or if flavouring cream with chocolate, simmer it in remaining milk until melted, then pour it on to egg mixture, blend and return it to pan.

Stir over gentle heat until the mixture boils.

Watchpoint The pastry cream must be smooth before it boils; if lumps form as it thickens, draw pan off heat, beat cream until smooth. If it is too stiff, add a little extra milk.

Whip the egg white until stiff, turn a little of the boiling cream into a bowl and fold in egg white. Return this to the pan and stir carefully for 2-3 minutes over the heat to set the egg white. Turn cream into a bowl to cool. If flavouring cream with coffee essence, stir it into the cooled cream.

Praline

2 oz almonds (unblanched)
2 oz caster sugar

Method
Put almonds and sugar into a small pan and cook slowly to a nut brown.

Stir well with a metal spoon when the sugar starts to brown. Then turn on to an oiled tin to cool. (See photograph, page 116.)

Crush the cooled praline with a rolling pin, or grind it in a nut mill, then sieve it. Store in an airtight container and use as required.

White praline

8 oz (240 g) lump sugar
8 fl oz water
4 oz (120 g) ground almonds

Sugar thermometer

Method
Dissolve sugar in water quickly to 250°F. Remove pan from heat, add almonds and stir mixture until sandy in texture. Pass it through a wire sieve, store in a screw-top jar.

Purées

Apricot purée
To prepare a purée from fresh apricots, take a sugar syrup made with ¾ cup water and 2 rounded tablespoons granulated sugar. Wipe and split the fruit, remove the stone and place fruit rounded side down in a pan. Add syrup and bring very slowly to the boil. Allow syrup to boil up and over the fruit, then reduce heat, cover pan and simmer very gently until tender. Strain, and rub fruit through a sieve. Thin purée if desired with the poaching juice.

To prepare a purée from dried apricots, first soak the fruit overnight, then cook until tender in the soaking liquid. Purée as above.

Strawberry purée
Hull strawberries and rub through a fine nylon sieve, or blend them in a liquidiser.

Redcurrant jelly

It is not possible to give a specific quantity of redcurrants as the recipe is governed by the amount of juice made, which is variable.

Method
Wash the fruit and, without removing from the stems, put in a 7 lb jam jar or stone crock. Cover and stand in deep pan of hot water. Simmer on top of the stove or in the oven at 350°F or Mark 4, mashing the fruit from time to time, until all the juice is extracted (about 1 hour).

Then turn fruit into a jelly-bag, or double linen strainer, and allow to drain undisturbed overnight over a basin.

Watchpoint To keep the jelly clear and sparkling, do not try to speed up the draining process by forcing juice through; this will only make the jelly cloudy.

Now measure juice. Allowing 1 lb lump or preserving sugar to each pint of juice, mix juice and sugar together, dissolving over slow heat. When dissolved, bring to the boil, boil hard for 3-5 minutes and skim with a wooden spoon. Test a little on a saucer: allow jelly to cool, tilt saucer and, if jelly is set, it will wrinkle. Put into jam jars, place small circles of greaseproof paper over jelly, label and cover with jam pot covers. Store in a dry larder until required.

Rice

To boil rice
Most people have their own favourite method of boiling rice. That recommended by Asians is to cook the rice in a small quantity of boiling water until this is absorbed, when rice is soft. The amount of water varies according to the quality of the rice. This method is good but

can present problems. Really the simplest way is to cook the rice (2 oz washed rice per person) in plenty of boiling, well-salted water (3 quarts per 8 oz rice) for about 12 minutes. You can add a slice of lemon for flavour. Stir with a fork to prevent rice sticking while boiling, and watch that it does not overcook.

To stop rice cooking, either tip it quickly into a colander and drain, or pour ½ cup cold water into the pan and then drain. Pour over a jug of hot water to wash away the remaining starch, making several holes through the rice with the handle of a wooden spoon to help it drain more quickly.

To reheat: spoon into a buttered ovenproof dish, cover with buttered paper, put in oven at 350°F or Mark 4 for 30 minutes.

With a pilaf, the rice is cooked in stock until it has been absorbed and the rice is dry and flaky. Though this can be done over a flame, it is best to put the pan or casserole in the oven to get both top and bottom heat.

Salad dressings

French dressing

1 tablespoon vinegar (red or white wine, cider, or tarragon)
3 tablespoons olive oil, or ground-nut oil
½ teaspoon salt
½ teaspoon black pepper (ground from mill)
good pinch of sugar (optional)

Method
Mix the vinegar with the seasonings, add the oil and when the dressing thickens, taste for correct seasoning. More salt should be added if the dressing is sharp yet oily.

Vinaigrette dressing
Make as for French dressing, but add a pinch of fresh chopped herbs (thyme, basil, marjoram, parsley).

Mayonnaise

2 egg yolks
salt and pepper
dry mustard
¾ cup of salad oil
2 tablespoons wine vinegar

This recipe will make ½ pint of mayonnaise.

Method
Work egg yolks and seasonings with a small whisk or wooden spoon in a bowl until thick; then start adding the oil drop by drop. When 2 tablespoons of oil have been added this mixture will be very thick. Now carefully stir in 1 teaspoon of the vinegar.

The remaining oil can then be added a little more quickly, either 1 tablespoon at a time and beaten thoroughly between each addition until it is absorbed, or in a thin steady stream if you are using an electric beater.

When all the oil has been absorbed, add remaining vinegar to taste, and extra salt and pepper as necessary.

To thin and lighten mayonnaise add a little hot water. For a coating consistency, thin with a little cream or milk.

Eggs should not come straight from the refrigerator. If oil is cloudy or chilled, it can be slightly warmed which will lessen the chances of eggs curdling. Put oil bottle in a pan of hot water for a short time.

Watchpoint Great care must be taken to prevent mayonnaise curdling. Add oil drop by drop at first, and then continue very slowly.

If mayonnaise curdles, start with a fresh yolk in another bowl and work well with seasoning, then add the curdled mixture to it very slowly and carefully. When curdled mixture is completely incorporated, more oil can be added if the mixture is too thin.

Sauces

Béchamel sauce

½ pint milk
1 slice of onion
1 small bayleaf
6 peppercorns
1 blade mace
¾ oz butter
½ oz plain flour
salt and pepper

Method
Put onion and spices in the milk and heat gently, without boiling, in a covered saucepan for 5-7 minutes.

Pour off into a jug and wipe out the pan. Melt the butter in this, and stir in the flour off the heat. Strain in a good third of the milk, blend and add remaining milk. When thoroughly mixed, season lightly, return to the heat and stir continually until boiling. Boil for 2-3 minutes, then adjust the seasoning.

Mock hollandaise sauce

2 oz butter
1 tablespoon plain flour
½ pint water (boiling)
1-2 egg yolks
salt and pepper
good squeeze of lemon juice

Method
Melt a good ½ oz of butter in a pan, stir in the flour off the heat and when smooth pour on all the boiling water, stirring or whisking briskly all the time.

Now add egg yolks and remaining butter in small pieces, stirring it well in. Season and add lemon juice. **Watchpoint** If the water is really boiling it will cook flour. On no account bring sauce to the boil as this will give it an unpleasant gluey taste.

Shellfish, preparation

Mussels
Mussels must be tightly closed before cooking. Examine carefully during the first thorough rinsing in cold water, and sharply tap any that are not tightly closed with the handle of a knife. If they do not respond by closing, discard them.

Scrub the mussels well with a small stiff brush and pull or scrape away any small pieces of weed from the sides. Rinse under a running tap, then soak them in a bowl of fresh water; do not tip this water off the mussels as this might leave sand still in them, but lift them into another bowl or colander and wash again. When thoroughly clean, lift them out and put into a large pan for cooking.

If mussels have to be kept overnight, store in a bowl without water in a cool place and cover them with a heavy damp cloth.

If storing mussels for a day or two, cover them with cold sea-water (if available) after washing and add a good tablespoon of oatmeal. This will feed them and keep them plump.

Scallops
Scallops when alive, have their shells tightly closed, but they are usually bought ready prepared (opened and cleaned).

The easiest way to open them yourself is to put the shells into a hot oven for 4-5 minutes. The heat will cause the shells to gape. You must then carefully scrape away the fringe or beard which surrounds the scallop, attached to the flat shell, and the black thread (the intestine) which lies round it.

Slip a sharp knife under the scallop to detach it and the roe from shell. Scallops must be handled carefully as the roe is delicate.

Scrub each shell thoroughly; these make good dishes to serve scallops in and can be used several times over.

Scallops take only 6-7 minutes to cook and, like all shellfish, should be simmered—not boiled (which makes them tough and tasteless). They can also be baked, fried or grilled.

Stocks

Brown bone stock

3 lb beef bones (or mixed beef/veal)
2 onions (quartered)
2 carrots (quartered)
1 stick of celery
large bouquet garni
6 peppercorns
3-4 quarts water
salt.

6-quart capacity saucepan, or small fish kettle

Method
Wipe bones but do not wash unless unavoidable. Put into a very large pan. Set on gentle heat and leave bones to fry gently for 15-20 minutes. Enough fat will come out from the marrow so do not add any to pan unless bones are very dry.

After 10 minutes add the vegetables, having sliced the celery into 3-4 pieces.

When bones and vegetables are just coloured, add herbs, peppercorns and the water, which should come up two-thirds above level of ingredients. Bring slowly to the boil, skimming occasionally, then half cover pan to allow reduction to take place and simmer 4-5 hours, or until stock tastes strong and good.

Chicken stock
This should ideally be made from the giblets (neck, gizzard, heart and feet, if available), but never the liver which imparts a bitter flavour. This is better kept for making pâté, or sautéd and used as a savoury. Dry fry the giblets with an onion, washed but not peeled, and cut in half. To dry fry, use a thick pan with a lid, with barely enough fat to cover the bottom. Allow the pan to get very hot before putting in the giblets and onion, cook on full heat until lightly coloured. Remove pan from heat before covering with 2 pints of cold water. Add a large pinch of salt, a few peppercorns and a bouquet garni (bayleaf, thyme, parsley) and simmer gently for 1-2 hours. Alternatively, make the stock when you cook the chicken by putting the giblets in the roasting tin around the chicken with the onion and herbs, and use the measured quantity of water.

Sugar syrup

Dissolve 1 lb lump, or granulated, sugar in ½ pint water and boil steadily, without stirring, until sugar thermometer reads 220°F. If storing, allow syrup to cool and pour it into a large, clean and dry screw-top jar.

Tomatoes

To skin tomatoes: place them in a bowl, scald by pouring boiling water over them, count 12, then pour off the hot water and replace it with cold. The skin then comes off easily.

Glossary

Bake blind To pre-cook a pastry case before filling it (see page 104 for method).

Blanch To whiten meats and remove strong tastes from vegetables by bringing to the boil from cold water and draining before further cooking. Green vegetables should be put into boiling water and cooked for up to 1 minute.

Egg wash Made by beating 1 egg with ½ teaspoon salt. This liquefies the egg, which makes it easier to brush a thin film on pastry, and increases the shine when baked.

Fécule Arrowroot or potato flour.

Used as a liaison for thickening sauces.

Infuse To steep in liquid (not always boiling) in a warm place, to draw flavour into the liquid.

Macerate To soak/infuse, mostly fruit, in liqueur/syrup.

Shortening Fat which when worked into flour gives a 'short' crisp quality to pastry/cakes. Fats with least liquid, eg. lard, vegetable fats, contain most shortening power.

Vanilla sugar Sugar delicately flavoured with vanilla (made by storing 1-2 vanilla pods in a jar of sugar).

Index

157